Dave
Thanks for keeping us informed.
Cam Re

 W9-AHA-394

YOUR ~~PRIVATE~~ PUBLIC IDENTITY

YOUR ~~PRIVATE~~ PUBLIC IDENTITY

BECAUSE NOTHING IS PRIVATE ANYMORE

CARRIE KERSKIE

DEDICATION

To my loving husband, Scott, and our amazing children, Kyle and Gwen, for always encouraging me to pursue my dreams, for giving me the opportunity to reach my dreams, and for standing by me as those dreams become reality.

To my dear family and friends for encouraging me to write this book.

CONTENTS

CONTENTS

WHY THIS BOOK WAS WRITTEN

I am an identity theft expert and on three separate occasions, I have been an identity theft victim. The first time occurred when my debit card was compromised by a data security breach from a grocery store chain. A data security breach occurs when sensitive information, data, has been exposed by either error or malicious intent. The second time involved a credit card that was set up for monthly billing from a company that experienced a data security breach. I knew it was this company, even though they never announced the breach, because I kept this particular card under lock and key, and only used it for services provided by the company in question. Since then, I have learned that other subscribers experienced breaches to their credit cards around the same time. The third time was when I was a patient at a local hospital where an employee sold patient files to another person for profit. At no time was there anything I could have done to have prevented the identity theft from happening. Sure, if I had paid by cash I could have prevented the first two, but the third one was completely out of my control.

I make my living as a private investigator, and in that role I have helped numerous victims of identity theft. I have also observed similar patterns and habits that lead to each client's becoming an ID theft victim. Because of this, I decided to offer presentations on identity theft as a service to my community to help others from making the same mistakes. Three years and two hundred presentations later, and after much encouragement from presentation attendees, I have written this book, which contains all of the information from my presentations, as well as additional resources to help you reduce your risk and monitor for suspicious activity. After reading this book, you will know what steps to take when you become a victim, and how to do it for little to no money.

In my career I have observed just how much information is available to anyone on the Internet as long as they know where to look. I have been able to prove fraud just by viewing a social networking profile. I have been able to prove fraud by accessing a website the criminal believed to be deleted from the Internet. I can also find out just about anything on just about anyone through a few simple free Internet searches. This is how your private identity has now become your *public* identity. By having a public identity, you now have a greater risk of becoming a victim of identity theft.

Identity theft can happen to anyone, anywhere, at anytime. Unfortunately, there is no way to prevent it from ever happening to you. There are many companies that promise to "prevent" identity theft but, as you will learn from this book, prevention is mission impossible.

Since identity theft cannot be prevented, what can you do? You can reduce your risk of becoming a victim by using the tips, tricks and techniques in this book. By understanding where your personal identifying information is located, who has access to it, and what can be done with it, you will reduce your risk of being a victim. You can monitor your information for little to no money. By monitoring your information, you will be able to detect any suspicious activity, be prepared to take action, and reduce your liability after you have become a victim.

This book will scare you and make you angry. But most importantly, it will open your eyes to exactly what is identity theft, how it occurs and what you can do to reduce your risk.

YOUR ~~PRIVATE~~ PUBLIC IDENTITY

PRIVACY IS DEAD

Not so long ago you were able to maintain your privacy. If your boss wanted to know who you had dinner with last night, he had to ask. If your children wanted to hear stories about the type of person you were in high school, they had to try to drag it out of your best friend or sibling. If your client wanted to know what you really thought about him, he would have to eavesdrop on your gossiping. Not so today. Thanks to advances in technology we now have the Internet, social networking, blogging, tweeting, email, and texting. People can find out more about you then you might realize. Right now, your personal identifying information is floating around in cyberspace. It is being shared by friends and family, shared by companies, and even shared by criminals. Just think about how many times you have used your name, address, telephone number and date of birth to create an account online. If you are not an online consumer, how many times you have been asked to provide your social security number, your driver's license number, or have completed a contest entry form? Or better yet, do you own property or own a vehicle? If you answered yes to any of these your identity has now become public.

"But how?" you ask. All of that information is being stored on a computer or in a file cabinet. If someone knows where to look and how to get it they can have information on you in mere seconds. How do I know? Because I can do it, and have done it thousands of times. However, I am not the one you need to be worried about, unless of course you are committing fraud. I have no intention of using your information to steal your identity. But, there are millions, make that **billions,** of criminals you SHOULD be worried about. These people spend all of their time searching for your information. They operate like a well-run corporation and create business plans on how to steal your information. Once found, they will use it to steal your money, steal your identity and destroy everything that you have worked so hard to obtain in your life.

Right now you are probably saying to yourself, "What can I do?" Well for starters, you bought this book. Step one - complete. As I said, I too can access your floating information and I am going to show you how it is done and where to find it yourself. But first, you need to think like a criminal. You need to get inside of his head to understand his motives, his techniques. Now I am not talking about a murderer, I am talking about an identity theft criminal. A person that will assume your identity to steal your money, ruin your credit or destroy your reputation. Once you truly understand how an identity theft criminal thinks, you will be able to greatly reduce your risk of becoming a victim.

Did you notice I said "reduce your risk" and not "prevent?" PREVENTION IS IMPOSSIBLE! That is a fact and if anyone tries to tell you differently run away because they are trying to sell you snake oil. *For those of you who don't know what snake oil is, it is a reference to a time when con artists would try to sell you dirt and tell you it was the fountain of youth.* I know you have seen the television ads saying they can "protect your identity" and it will only cost you $9.95 a month. I can tell you they will protect you as well as that dirt will keep you young forever - but more on identity theft prevention services in another chapter.

Now let's get back to how this book will help you. Section one, *Identity Theft*, will help you see identity theft from the mind of a criminal. You will learn the six types of identity theft, (Yes, I said six), what they are, why they happen, how they happen, how it effects you and case examples. I must warn you, this section will scare you. My intention is to open your eyes. Far too often I see people living in their own little worlds until they become a victim. At that point they say, "But why did this happen to me"? The answer is simple: because they were too scared to look at the big picture.

Section two, *How to Avoid Becoming a Victim*, digs deeper into how criminals get your information. Not only do they get it from the Internet, often it is provided by the victim himself. I am not talking by armed robbery, I am talking about the everyday things you do. After this section you will see for yourself all of the ways you too are personally giving your information to criminals. If the first section did not scare you this one will. During my presentations it is at this point that I typically pass out the antacids as attendees are feeling a bit nauseous. Again, my intention is not to scare you, but to make you aware of the common mistakes made by victims. While reading this section, make notes (on worksheet at the end of the section) of all of the mistakes you are currently making. Just make sure you are honest and do not be discouraged. I have yet to meet anyone that has not found at least one mistake they are currently making. This will help you determine areas to focus on in section three.

Section three, *Get Proactive*, gives you the tips, tricks and techniques to greatly reduce your risk of becoming an identity theft victim. (Remember, prevention is impossible.) I recommend you first read this entire section in its entirety. Once completed, re-read the areas that offer solutions to the mistakes you noted from section two. Do this before starting Section four. Take your time to implement each step and use the worksheet at the end of the section.

Once you have implemented the proactive steps, proceed to Section four, *Warning Signs*, which will provide you with the common warning signs of identity theft. If, while reading this section, you find you have observed a warning sign(s), make a note on the worksheet at the end of Section four and keep reading. Keep in mind, the more warning signs, the greater the chance you may already be a victim.

Section five, *I'm a Victim, Now What*, provides you with the steps to take to prevent further damage and to begin to restore your identity. This section also provides you with an easy-to-use checklist to guide you each step of the way.

Section six, *Deadlines to Remember*, discusses laws that can greatly impact your wallet. For example, did you know that how you use your combination debit/credit card determines your maximum out of pocket liability? You will also learn how to get free credit reports and more. This section alone can save you up to $200 by implementing one technique.

Section seven, *A Closer Look at ID Protection Services*, takes a look at four types of identity theft prevention services offered by various companies. Each service is broken down by pros and cons so that you can make an informed decision before paying for the service. Some of these services are great and can save you a lot of time and money, while others are a complete waste of money. Before you buy an identity theft prevention service read this section.

Section eight, *How to Self Monitor*, provides you with tips, tricks and techniques to continue to monitor your personal identifying information. If you thought that all you had to do was read this book once and you were done, think again. Reducing your risk of identity theft is a continuous task. This section will help to make it easier by providing you with contacts, timelines, and worksheets to document your activities.

As a bonus for purchasing this book, in this section you will find a code that will provide you with access to all of the worksheets, contacts and more in downloadable form or easy to use links.

So grab a cup of coffee, find a comfortable chair and start reading.

THE FACTS ABOUT IDENTITY THEFT

I remember the first time I offered to speak to a local organization, for free, to educate their members on the dangers of identity theft. The woman on the phone replied, "I'm sorry, but identity theft does not happen in Naples, Florida." I was shocked, confused and amazed at just how uninformed this woman was about identity theft and just how frequently it occurs. I wanted to make sure that I was prepared the next time someone made the same statement, so I contacted my local sheriff's department and requested a report on the number of reported cases of identity theft for 2007. The report indicated there were 321 reported cases of identity theft. Now this may not sound like a lot but consider this: 65% of identity theft cases never get reported to law enforcement.

I knew this would not be enough to convince others, such as the woman on the phone, that identity theft was a problem and on the rise. I started researching everything I could about identity theft statistics. Here are the results of my investigation:

Javelin Strategy & Research

- 11.3 million adults were victims of identity theft in 2009.
- The number of identity theft victims increased by 12% and the amount of fraud increased 12.5% in 2009. This is the highest reported increase in seven years.
- 1 in every 10 U.S. consumers has been victimized by identity theft.
- 50.2 million Americans use credit monitoring. (September 2008).

- 25.9 million Americans carry identity theft insurance. (September 2008).

US Department of Justice (2005)

- Identity theft has surpassed drug trafficking in the United States.
- 1.6 million American households have experienced fraud not related to credit cards.
- Households with incomes higher than $75, 000 are twice as likely to experience identity theft than those with incomes less than $50,000.
- The dollar amount lost per household averages $1,620.

Identity Theft Resource Center Aftermath Research 2009

- 38-48% of victims discovered the incident within three months.
- 9-18% took four or more years to discover they were a victim of identity theft.
- The average identity theft victim spends 300 hours repairing the damage.
- More than 35 million data records were compromised by corporate and government data breaches in 2008.

Ponemon Institute

- In 2009 there were 1.5 million reported cases of medical identity theft, representing and estimated cost of $28.6 billion.
- The average cost to resolve the issue was $20,000 (the equivalent of over 110 years of our service at $14.95 per month) and more than 50% had to pay for care not received to restore their insurance coverage.
- 48% lost health insurance as a result of the incident and 36% reported an increase in their health insurance premiums.

Aberdeen Group

Businesses globally lost $221 billion a year to identity theft.

From these statistics it is easy to see that identity theft is on the rise, can occur at anytime, anywhere and to anyone.

SIX TYPES OF IDENTITY THEFT

You are probably familiar with the most common type of identity theft, financial, but did you know there are actually six types of identity theft?

They are

- Financial
- Utilities
- Government documents and benefits
- Medical
- Criminal
- Business

There are few identity theft experts who discuss business identity theft, but as a private investigator I have worked with businesses which were affected and the owners will tell you that it is very real.

Each of these types will be discussed in detail explaining what they are, with information on actual cases to show you how they occur.

Financial Identity Theft

What is It?

Financial identity theft is when someone uses your identity to gain access to your finances or your financial reputation, better know as your credit. Financial identity theft is the type most individuals are familiar with because it's talked about in the media the most. There are many venues financial identity theft occurs including, but not limited to, credit cards, bank accounts, mortgages and bankruptcy.

CREDIT CARDS

Credit card identity theft occurs when someone either uses your current credit card or obtains a new credit card in your name for purchases.

Why It is Done

MONEY! Criminals want money and will use your credit to get it. They make purchases using your credit and then sell the merchandise for cash. Sometimes, criminals will use your credit to hide their true identity when purchasing illegal merchandise, such as child pornography. People in this country illegally will also use your credit because they are not able to obtain their own credit.

How They Do It

Steal your wallet or purse -There was a crime gang that would pick pocket at major events, take the stolen credit cards to a van parked outside, mass produce the credit cards and distribute them to their members to make as many purchases as possible all while you are enjoying the event.

Use a discarded credit card application - The criminal fills out the pre-approved application and sends it to the credit card company. Often times the account is approved and now they have a brand new credit card in your name, using your credit.

Skimmer device - A handheld device that captures all of the information stored on the magnetic strip on the back of your credit card or debit card. This information is then used to make counterfeit copies of your credit card or debit card. Criminals will use these in restaurants, on fuel pumps and at ATM's. Additional information on skimmers will be discussed Section two of this book.

How It Affects You

- Negatively impacts your credit rating.
- Can cause you to be denied credit, have your current credit limit reduced or suspended.
- Force you to pay out of pocket for purchases you did not make.

Case Example

A couple was attempting to purchase their first home. They found the perfect property and met with their bank, which ran their credit reports and observed an unpaid account on the husband's credit report. The man was surprised, as he had always paid his credit cards in full when due. He reviewed a copy of his credit report and noticed an account with a company he had never before done business. After contacting the company and a lengthy investigation, he discovered that someone, a family member, had applied for the account using his name.

BANK ACCOUNTS

Bank account identity theft occurs when someone uses your identity to either open a bank account in your name or to gain access to the funds in your current bank account. Bank accounts include, checking, savings, loans (auto or mortgage), lines of credit and investments such as CD's and mutual funds.

Why It is Done

Two reasons: to get your money or because the person cannot open a bank account himself. If someone is illegal, a wanted criminal, has a history of multiple bounced checks, poor credit, or is attempting to hide assets, he will need your identity to get a bank account.

How They Do It

Check washing - A chemical is used to remove the written ink off of the face of a check. Typically the "pay to" and "amount" are washed off leaving the signature. Then, the criminal writes completes the washed sections. Check washing will be covered again in Section two.

Steal your mail - When you pay a bill, put it in the mailbox and raise the little red flag it is a signal to criminals to "come and get it." Now they have your check, your bank information and your account number. Depending on what bill you were paying they could have even more information. They don't even have to wait for the flag. All they have to do is open the mailbox to find your brand new box of checks you ordered from the bank along with this month's statement.

Just be you - With the information accessed online or purchased online for a few dollars a criminal can create a counterfeit driver's license with all of your information and their picture. They can also get your social security number and date of birth. These are then used to open a new account in your name.

How It Affects You

- Negatively affect your Chexsystem report.

- Negatively effect your credit rating when the criminal's loan is not paid (auto loan or mortgage foreclosure).

- Money is stolen directly from your account.

Case Example

An elderly woman had all of her accounts at one bank. She also had auto draft protection linking her accounts. The woman was ill and hospitalized. Upon her return home, she discovered a letter from her bank demanding she pay thousands of dollars in overdraft fees. Assuming this was just a simple mistake she called her bank and learned that all of her bank accounts were empty. An investigation was launched which revealed someone had gained access to one of her accounts, her checking account, and had been writing checks against it.

Once the checking account was depleted her overdraft kicked in and the other accounts were soon depleted as well. Each time a transfer was made from her other accounts to her checking account, an overdraft fee was charged. This woman's life savings was stolen and now she was faced with thousands of dollars in overdraft fees for something she did not do. To make matters worse, because of the agreement with the bank she was responsible for the fees and the bank did not have to replace the stolen money.

BANKRUPTCY

Bankruptcy identity theft occurs when someone files for bankruptcy in your name.

Why It is Done

Now you might be asking yourself, what benefit would a criminal have by filing bankruptcy in your name? Let me explain. Not all identity theft is done to steal your personal money. Identity theft is also used when a person is in this country illegally or is a wanted fugitive. They just need an alias so they can go about their life undetected. They find your identity and become you, on paper. They pay their bills, open bank accounts, obtain loans and a mortgage and, in past investigations, have actually increased a victim's credit rating. But then something happens and the bills can no longer be paid. They do what many people do in this type of situation: they file for bankruptcy. The only difference is that the bankruptcy is filed in their alias, your identity.

How They Do It

They simply file for bankruptcy using your social security number, name and date of birth. They have been living under your identity for quite some time and have accounts to support their claim of being you.

How It Affects You

When a person files for bankruptcy they have to provide a financial statement documenting ALL assets. Of course the criminal only knows of his own assets accumulated while using your identity and your own personal assets are not listed. When a due diligence investigation for assets is conducted, your own personal assets are located and you are sent a notice from the courts stating your assets have been frozen. You are also put on notice that you attempted to defraud the government by not disclosing ALL of your assets. Remember the criminal only listed his assets accumulated while using *your* identity.

Case Example

This is exactly what happened to another elderly woman. She received notification that her assets were being frozen and she was under investigation for bankruptcy fraud. Further investigation revealed that someone had been using her identity for many years in another state. The criminal paid the bills, purchased vehicles, and a residence all using the elderly woman's identity. Then the economy shifted. The criminal was unable to keep up with the bills and in order to keep up the charade, filed for bankruptcy using the identity of the elderly woman. Until the elderly woman was notified by the courts, she had no idea her identity was being used by another person. There were no warning signs, such as collection calls or unknown charges on her credit card, or denials of credit because the criminal paid her bills. This went undetected because it was done in another state and the elderly woman never reviewed her credit report. If she would have requested a copy of her credit report she would have observed the multiple accounts and addresses that were not hers.

Utilities Identity Theft

What Is It?

Utilities identity theft occurs when someone uses your identity to gain access to utilities such as power, cable television, water or telephone - whether landline and cellular.

Why It is Done

When a new account is established for utilities the company will sometimes run a credit report before offering services. If the credit rating is too low then they may impose a high deposit or deny service. Someone may use your identity to gain service and avoid the high deposit. They may also be motivated to use your identity if they are a wanted criminal or are in this country illegally.

How They Do It

When a criminal applies for utilities they simply provide your personal identifying information to the utilities company. It is that easy. If an ID is required, for around $50 a criminal can purchase a counterfeit driver's license or make it himself. States have been attempting to prevent this by creating holograms and watermarks, but unfortunately these criminals are typically ten steps ahead of the government.

How It Affects You

When the criminal stops paying the utility bill it is turned over to collections. This will have a direct impact on your credit rating. You may also loose your service due to an unpaid balance on another account.

Case Example

A local man was moving from one residence to another within the same town. He contacted the local power company to change the address of his service but was told he would first need to pay the outstanding balance. When he told the power company he does not have an outstanding balance for his old address. The power company told him the balance was for another address, an address where he had never lived. After further research it was revealed that the man's former roommate had been using his identity for three years and they had both been living in the same town.

Government Documents and Benefits

What Is It?

Government documents and benefits identity theft occurs when someone uses your identity to duplicate government documents and/or receive government benefits. Examples of this would be duplicating a Social Security card; driver's license; state issued ID; or applying for and receiving Medicare, Medicaid, or disability or Social Security benefits in your name.

Why It is Done

There are numerous reasons why this is done but the most common is for financial gain or to conceal the criminal's true identity.

How They Do It

Counterfeit social security cards and driver's licenses can be purchased on the streets and online for around $50. As I said before, your information is already out there. You don't know where it is, or who has access to it - but the criminals do. Once someone has your Social Security number, name and date of birth they can assume your identity.

How It Affects You

- **Social Security Card:** Allows the criminal to apply for work, secure credit, and more. When they do not file a tax return for the income earned you are the one that receives the notice from the IRS. When they stop paying the bills it is your credit that is affected.
- **Driver's license:** Allows the criminal to rack up points on your license for his poor driving habits; allows him to pose as you when applying for a job, establishing credit, visiting a doctor and more. This will be discussed further in the chapter on Criminal Identity Theft.
- **Medicare/Medicaid:** Allows the criminal to use your benefits. This will be discussed further in the chapter on Medical Identity Theft.

- **Social Security benefits**: Allows the criminal to apply for benefits in your name prior to you filing for benefits. It could also allow him to continue to receive benefits after someone has died.

Case Example

A man filed his tax return, as required, reporting all of his income. He later received a notice from the IRS inquiring about additional income not reported on his return. The man believed it was a mistake since he did not have any other sources of income. Further research revealed that someone using his Social Security number had obtained employment and received income. When the employer filed the W-2 with the Social Security number on file it triggered an alert with the IRS since the criminal had not filed a tax return. If the criminal had filed a tax return this would have also raised a red flag, as two separate tax returns would have been filed in the same Social Security number.

Medical Identity Theft

What Is It?

Medical identity theft occurs when someone uses your identity to obtain medical services or medical products, such as prosthetics or wheelchairs. It is the fastest growing form of identity theft and is the deadliest. Very few American have ever heard of medical identity theft until they themselves become a victim.

Why It is Done

When a criminal needs medical treatment and either does not have insurance, is illegal, is a wanted fugitive, or wants to conceal his ailment, he will assume your identity and obtain the services and/or products under your identity. He is treated for free and you and your insurance company are left to pay the bills.

But medical services and/or products are not the only reason. The second reason is, once again, money. Unfortunately there are few checks and balances in the healthcare industry which allows criminals to manipulate the system, stealing billions of dollars a year from American taxpayers. It is estimated that in 2009, $60 billion was lost due to Medicare fraud alone.

How They Do It

Criminals will steal the credentials of healthcare providers, set up an account with Medicare, purchase a list of patient names, addresses, dates of birth and social security numbers, and set up a computer program to automatically submit fraudulent claims to Medicare.

This has also been done by healthcare providers themselves. They will submit additional claims, in your name, and be paid for additional services and/or products, you did not receive. This is why it is so important to review your Explanation of Benefits that you receive from your health insurance carrier or Medicaid. The Explanation of Benefits (EOB) shows you what claims have been paid, the date of service, and the healthcare provider submitting the claim.

How It Affects You

- You are billed for the co-pay for services rendered to the criminal.
- When the bills are not paid, they are turned over to collections and are reflected on your credit report.
- Your medical record is now commingled with the information and diagnosis of the criminal.
- If the criminal is diagnosed with cancer, HIV, or diabetes it is noted on your permanent medical record.
- Your health insurance premiums may rise.
- You may lose your health insurance coverage.
- The criminal can exhaust all of your health insurance benefits.
- If your medical record reflects a diagnosis such as diabetes, cancer, etc., then you will not be able to obtain additional health or live insurance as you are now labeled "high risk."
- You could be misdiagnosed due to misinformation in your medical record.
- You could be given the wrong blood type because the criminal's blood type is now in your medical record.
- Once you tell a healthcare provider, "It was not me that received the services, treatment, etc." you are no longer allowed access to that medical record, even if it is your medical record, because HIPAA – the healthcare privacy law- prohibits it.
- It could cost you your life.

Case Example

The best case example I found was not a case I was directly involved with, but one I discovered in a news report a couple of years ago. The reason I am using this one is because if it was not documented by others you would think it was fabricated.

Florida resident Linda Weaver received a bill from the hospital for a foot amputation. She knew this was an error since both her feet were intact. She contacted the hospital and was told that the bill was still her responsibility.

She contacted her insurance company thinking they would be

able to help her. Once the insurance company learned it was not her and that fraud was involved, it rescinded payment to the hospital, which then billed Weaver for the full cost of the surgery.

Ms. Weaver demanded to see the patient file but was refused due to HIPAA laws. (Remember, she told them it was not her.) She raised such a fit in the hospital that hospital workers allowed her to view the patient file which indicated she had diabetes. She does not. Ms. Weaver noted which information in her patient file belonged to the woman who fraudulently used her identity thinking it would be removed from her file.

The hospital bills were turned over to collections for non-payment which began to destroy her credit rating.

Some time later, Ms. Weaver suffered a heart attack. Wonder why, perhaps stress related? While in the hospital the nurse asked her what diabetes medication she was taking. Ms. Weaver was shocked, she thought she had separated the misinformation from her patient file but, here it was, still in her patient file.

Now remember the claim was that she had her foot amputated. Anyone with working eyes could clearly see she had both of her feet. How much more obvious can you get to prove she did not have the surgery? Unfortunately, the laws written to protect us are working against us, as it did for Linda Weaver. Her identity was used, so she was responsible for the bills. She said "it was not me" and was denied access to her own patient file.

This can happen to anyone, anywhere. In addition, by the time you receive a warning sign, an EOB or call from a collection agency, the damage has been done, typically twelve to fourteen months earlier.

Criminal Identity Theft

What Is It?

Criminal identity theft occurs when someone presents law enforcement with your identity when violating the law. This can be for traffic, misdemeanors or felonies. People often say to me, "But the fingerprints will not match." Well, unless you have been fingerprinted for a criminal act there will be not fingerprints on file for you. If the criminal is the first to be arrested and fingerprinted then *his* fingerprints become *your* fingerprints.

Why It is Done

If someone is a wanted criminal, has lost their driver's license due to poor driving habits, or in this country illegally they will use your identity as a cover. As the old saying goes, a leopard does not change its spots and soon enough the criminal will be arrested again, this time, they will present your identifying information.

How They Do It

Driver's licenses and Social Security numbers can be bought off the street or online for around $50. When an ID is stolen or lost it is mass produced and sold. Your information can also be located on the Internet or purchased from a data vendor.

How It Affects You

Simple: you will now have a criminal record or traffic record. When someone using your driver's license racks up enough points on your license, it is suspended. Now what happens when you are involved in a fender bender and the Officer informs you are driving on a suspended license? Or when your auto insurance carrier notifies you of a premium increase or denial of insurance?

This can also affect your ability to gain employment. My company conducts pre-employment background investigations for employers. We have observed an increase in the number of investigations that reveal a criminal record. When the employer asks the applicant about the record, the applicant is surprised as they have never lived in or visited the county of record. Further investigation revealed the applicant was telling the truth and the criminal has fraudulently used their identity.

Case Example

A man – let's call him Jim - drives to a gas station, places his wallet on the gas pump and fuels his vehicle. Jim drives away and later realizes he left his wallet on the pump. The wallet was stolen so he files a police report. A few weeks later he receives a call from the police department stating they had recovered a few of his personal articles and asked him to come down to the station. Upon Jim's arrival, he observes a table with bundled stacks of counterfeit driver's licenses, all with his information minus one item - a photograph. These had been mass produced to sell. But this story does not end here.

Jim also learns that someone who purchased one of these licenses, containing his information, had killed three people. So, Jim, the man who left his wallet on the fuel pump, now had a warrant for his arrest for the murder of three people. Jim now has to have his attorney on speed dial. Imagine what would happen if Jim was involved in a minor fender bender? The officer would run his license and see there was a warrant for his arrest for murder. What if his family was in the car at the time? Imagine the impact on his children as they watch officers arrest their father at gun point. All because Jim left his wallet on a fuel pump.

Business Identity Theft

What Is It?

Business identity theft occurs someone either assumes the identity of a business owner or the business as an entity, or when a purchase has been made by an identity theft criminal. When the owner of a small business is the victim of identity theft his credit is affected and so is the credit of the business. Until a business is able to obtain its own credit the owner's credit is used for purchases and such.

The business entity can be a victim of identity theft when a criminal uses your business's brand and identity to obtain money or information from its customers. It can also be a victim when the business's credentials are used to obtain a credit card, credit account or merchandise from a vendor.

Very few ID theft experts mention business identity theft, but as a private investigator, I have helped businesses that were victims. I have observed the damage it caused and the difficulty in restoring not only the business credit, but its reputation.

Businesses can also be the perpetrators of identity theft when they experience a data security breach. This means that your personal information, stored on their computers or in their files, has been exposed. Once exposed, you are now at risk for identity theft. Depending on the cause of the data breach your information may be sold to other criminals, unleashing a lifetime of battling identity theft.

Why It is Done

You guessed it - MONEY!!! These people want to take money from your customers, your vendors, or directly from your business. Once they have purchased merchandise from your vendor(s) they can sell it online or on the black market for cash - and you get the bill.

How They Do It

Business information can be obtained through a quick online search. Most states have an online directory for businesses registered in their state. Often times, these include the names and addresses of the business, owner(s) and the Federal tax ID number (FEIN). Criminals can also spoof your company website so your customers think they are on your website.

Criminals will dig through your trash in hopes of finding a discarded, pre-approved credit card application or other valuable bit of information; perhaps a voided check or a discarded tax return.

Criminals will make purchases from your business using stolen or counterfeit credit cards or debit cards, checks or other items. You provide them the product or service and try to collect your money. You soon discover the credit card or check was stolen and you can no longer collect for the product or provided service.

Business data security breaches can be as easy as an employee discarding customer or patient files into the dumpster, a company laptop being stolen, or as complicated as hacking into the company computer.

How It Affects You

- No longer able to obtain business credit.
- Lose vendors.
- Hurt or destroy your company's reputation.
- Lose customer confidence.
- Fewer customers leads to lost revenue.
- Providing products or services for free because you cannot collect payment from an ID theft victim.
- Lifetime dealings with identity theft occurrences.

Case Example

A business owner received an application for a corporate credit card in the mail. She did not want or need the credit card so she threw it away. A criminal found it, completed the application and received a credit card for the company. The criminal then began to make purchases and, of course, did not pay the bills. The business owner received a collections call from the credit card company for the unpaid balance. She was shocked because she did not apply for the corporate credit card. Further investigation revealed the source for the fraud was the thrown away credit card application.

Here's another example: a customer purchases $10,000 of merchandise from an upscale retail store using a stolen credit card. Unfortunately the purchases were made before the cardholder reported the card stolen. The transaction was approved and the customer left with $10,000 in merchandise. A few days later the credit card company rescinds the payment to the store because the card was reported stolen. The store owner is now out $10,000 in merchandise with no way to recover the money.

NOTES:

HOW TO AVOID BECOMING A VICTIM

Now that you have a better understanding of all of the ways your identity can be used, you need to understand how your information is obtained. This section will provide you with the most common mistakes which led others to becoming identity theft victims.

I have also provided you with a worksheet, at the end of this section, to track common mistakes that may be putting your identity at risk. This is not a test and is not a reflection on your intelligence. These are common everyday mistakes made by everyone at anytime. Be honest with yourself. It is the only way to reduce your risk. Make sure to have your family do the same. It only takes one person in your household to put everyone at risk.

Theft

Just as it sounds, criminals obtain your information by stealing an item with your personal identifying information. For a moment, look around and think of all of the items that have your personal identifying information. Are you looking at your purse or wallet? Are you looking at your computer, laptop or cell phone? You should be. But these are only a small portion of the items containing your personal identifying information. In fact, your personal identifying information is located on more items that are NOT in your possession then are in your possession: computers owned by companies where you have conducted business, file cabinets and microfilm storage facilities. As I said before, your information is out there, everywhere, and can be accessed by anyone who wants it bad enough.

You can't control the items not in your possession, so let's focus, for now, on the items you can control.

Purse/Wallet

What do you have right now in your purse or wallet? Your driver's license, your health insurance card, a credit card or two (or more), or maybe even a checkbook. Even without the checkbook, you have all of the ingredients a criminal needs to assume your identity. Even without your social security number. With the afore mentioned items, a criminal can easily obtain your social security number. Illegally, of course, but we are taking about someone who does not obey the laws.

By the time you realize your purse or wallet has been stolen, the criminal has already gone on a shopping spree with your credit cards. If the criminal is not savvy enough to know how to use the other items then he will sell them to another criminal who does.

Solutions

- Make a photocopy of everything you keep in your wallet, front and back.
- NEVER carry your Social Security Card.
- Only carry what you need, no extra credit cards.

- Have a low credit limit on the credit card you use everyday. This will make the criminal's shopping spree limited.
- Do not carry your ATM pin number with your ATM card.
- Do not leave your purse or wallet unattended, even for a second. Especially in shopping carts.
- Sign your credit card and write "See ID' near your signature. If you don't sign it, the criminal will and their signature now is the one that the store clerk will look at for comparison.

Unlocked Mailbox

As was mentioned before, if you are leaving bills in an unlocked mailbox they become fair game for criminals. At this very moment, there are criminals trolling neighborhoods opening mailboxes.

Solutions

Incoming mail-

Purchase a PO Box from the United States Postal Service (USPS). The fee is $44 per year, as of this writing, for a small box. Have all of your sensitive information (statements, new checks, credit cards) sent to the PO Box.

Purchase a USPS approved locking mailbox, which are available at your local hardware store or online. They typically start at around $150 and go up from there depending on size and design. This is a small price to pay in comparison to someone destroying your credit or stealing your hard earned money.

Outgoing mail-

Place your outgoing mail in a secured collection box provided by the USPS. These are the blue boxes scattered around your town or on site at your local USPS office. If you have a PO Box then just drop it in the collection box when you pick up your mail.

If you purchased a USPS approved locking mailbox then you can place the mail in the mailbox. The mailbox has a secured area that can be opened with a key by your postal carrier.

In Home Workers or Service Providers

These would include, but not limited to, an A/C repairman, a housekeeper, a babysitter, or a home remodeling crew.

If you have someone in your home and your sensitive information, such as bank and credit card statements, are on the kitchen table (or anywhere else), you are putting your information at risk. With cameras on cell phones, it takes mere seconds for someone to photograph the document and go on about their business. You have no idea it has been compromised as it is still in the same position you left it.

Also, if your supply of bank checks, or emergency credit cards, is not stored in a locked file cabinet or safe you are putting yourself at risk. When a criminal steals your checks, they do not steal the next set of checks they steal the one at the bottom or end. This way you do not realize the checks missing until many months or, depending on how fast you use them, years later. This is the same for older statements. You have already reconciled your statement and have filed them away. If it is not locked, then the criminal will take and old statement. They don't care about what you recently charged to your credit card. They only want the credit card number and your information.

The same can also be said for someone breaking into your home. Think about what sensitive information would be exposed if someone broke into your home right this minute. This is another reason to make it a habit of securing your sensitive information.

Solutions

- Secure all sensitive documents in a locked location.
- Do not leave the key in the file cabinet.
- Hide the key in a well hidden area. This does not include your junk drawer, desk drawer, or on top of the file cabinet.
- Before you let anyone, friends and family included, into your home secure all sensitive information.
- Monitor the activity of the worker until her or she is finished.
- Request criminal background checks are conducted on all workers before you allow them to enter your home. If the company refuses,

hire another company.

Home Computers

Your personal computer probably holds quite a bit of your personal information - information you would not want falling into the wrong hands. If your computer(s) are not password protected then anyone inside of your home can access the computer. This includes workers previously mentioned. It only takes mere seconds to download large amounts of data onto a portable USB storage device. These devices are so small it is easy concealed them in a pocket, tool belt, or keychain.

Another risk is your wireless router. This is the device that allows you to work from your laptop in any room. The signal from these routers can easily reach neighbors or anyone else near your home. If the router is not encrypted (password protected) then anyone in reach can get onto your network and into your computer(s). When a criminal drives up and down your neighborhood looking for unencrypted networks, this is known as war driving. This technique was used to steal credit card information from many large companies. Once the criminal is in your network he can upload a virus onto your computer and steal your information and remotely access your computer. This same technique is used by your neighbor to steal your Internet service. While your neighbor may not be accessing your information, he is still committing a crime.

Solution

- Password protect your computers.
- If using a screen saver, configure it so a password is needed to access the computer.
- Password protect (encrypt) your wireless router.
- Do not share your encryption key with others.

Pretexting

The definition of pretexting is "the practice of deceiving individuals into surrendering personal information for fraudulent purposes." There are many scams criminals use when pretexting.

Donations

Criminals will either create a fictitious charity or will use a legitimate charity in an attempt to get your money. It is best to decline donations by phone. Only donate to charities that you contact. Even if you have donated to the same charity in the past, do not give them any information by phone. A legitimate charity will understand your concerns.

A hospice became an unwitting accessory to a criminal ring's pretexing scam. The criminals would read obituaries, gather names of surviving family members and then send them a letter asking for a donation to the hospice center. This crime continued for quite some time until a suspicious family member notified the police, which then contacted the legitimate hospice center. Turns out, the hospice was not sending out donation letters.

You also need to be aware of telemarketers that are hired by charities to solicit donations. These are legitimate companies and typically are not attempting to steal your money. I bring them up because when you donate through these telemarketers, the charity does not receive your full donation. A portion of the donation, either a flat rate or percentage, is given to the telemarketer. Again, it is better to contact your charity of choice and make a donation directly to the organization.

Solutions

- Only make donations to charities you contact.
- Never give out credit card or bank information on calls that you did not initiate.
- When in doubt contact the charity directly to verify if they

contacted you.

- Ask if the caller works for the charity or a third party company.

Credit Card Alert

You receive a call from what appears to be your credit card company. They are calling because suspicious activity has been detected on your credit card and the company wants to help. The caller may even provide you with your account number, your mailing address and the name on the account. But you have something they don't, the three or four digit security code on the credit card. Either way, they were not able to capture your security code number and need it to make purchases. This may due to your information being obtained by a skimmer or from stealing your mail. Many have fallen for this scam, as the criminal has so much personal information already.

When a legitimate credit card company calls you to report suspicious activity, they do not ask you for sensitive information. They merely ask if you made a purchase at (or with) company X on such and such a date in the amount of Y. When you say no, they make a notation in your file. That is it!! If you have any doubts call the credit card company back, using the number on the back of your credit card, and ask to speak to the fraud department. They will be able to verify the call.

Solutions

- Never give out sensitive information on an uninitiated phone call.
- When in doubt contact the credit card company at the phone number on the back of your credit card or statement.
- If you are suspicious while on a call, tell the person you are busy and ask for their contact information to call them back. Then call the number on your credit card and ask for their department and name.

Survey

Criminals will call you asking you if you would mind answering a few questions. Oh, and this is my favorite part, "it will only take a minute of your time." The criminal will ask you a few questions about a product or service and then comes the good part. He will ask you for your name, your address and even for your date of birth and social security number. When questioned about the social security number they have a song and dance about how they use it to prove the survey is legitimate or so they know you have already participated. Yes, there are legitimate companies conducting surveys to help businesses improve their customer service or product, but not a single one of them will ever ask you for your social security number.

Another scenario is that your survey participation will be rewarded with an expensive prize. All you have to do is pay a small fee for taxes, shipping and whatever else they come up with. You send them your check, and guess what? The prize never appears. Now they have your bank account information and your money. Or you give them your credit card information to cover the fee. Next thing you know it there are tons of charges on your statement for purchases you did not authorize.

Rule of thumb: never participate in a survey when the survey taker is calling you.

Solutions

- Do not participate in phone surveys.
- If it is a prize, it will be free. No cost to you.
- Never send money for items in a call you did not initiate.
- Never provide your sensitive information in uninitiated calls.

Sales Call

Quite simply, someone tries to sell you something over the phone. Same motivation as with the survey. The criminal's objective is to get your credit card information or your check.

Solutions

- This one is an easy one to handle, just simply say you are not interested and hang up.
- Never provide your sensitive information in uninitiated calls.

Foreclosure Assistance

With the poor economy and the rising number of foreclosures it is easy to see how this one works. Unfortunately it works too well.

You receive a call from a company that promises to help you protect your home from foreclosure. Ultimately the motive is, again, money, but there are many techniques used to get the money. The caller may tell you that if you pay them, say, $1,500 they will stop the bank from foreclosing on your home. You send the money and the bank takes your home because this company did nothing. This so-called company didn't make one phone call on your behalf. It only wanted you send a check so these criminals could move to their next victim.

Another variation is to have you send money and sign a quick claim deed and the company will protect your home. Of course everything is either done online or through the mail. Now, not only are you out the money, you are also no longer the owner of your home, and you are still responsible for your mortgage.

Don't fall victim to these scams. If you are at risk of losing your home, do your research and search out legitimate companies to help you. Ask friends and family for a referral or contact your local Chamber of Commerce or Better Business Bureau.

Solutions

- Do not hire, contract or pay a company in an uninitiated call.
- Ask friends and family to recommend a legitimate company.
- Search the Internet for complaints against the company.
- Never provide your sensitive information in uninitiated calls.

Grants

If you get a call from someone saying you are entitled to receive a free grant hang up immediately. Grants are not handed out randomly nor or they given to individuals. The process of getting a grant is long and difficult. If it was easy, everyone would apply for them.

Solutions

- Hang up.
- Individuals are not awarded grants.

Contest Winner

This one has been around as long as there have been contests. The criminal calls you and says, in an excited voice, "Congratulations, you have won an all-expenses-paid vacation for two to the Caribbean!" *Wow, imagine that. I won a contest and I never even submitted an entry form. This must be my lucky day!!* Think again. As in the other types of pretexting, the criminal just wants your information or your money. You begin to realize this when you hear the familiar "all you have to do is pay a small fee to cover..." You know what happens if you fall for this. You give them your credit card information or you send them a check and then realize there is no vacation, no new car, or whatever else they told you won.

Solutions

- Hang up the phone.
- Prizes are free and do not cost you anything.
- Do not give them your sensitive information.
- You cannot win a contest you did not enter.

Family Member in Trouble

This one is much more personal and is often used with older persons. The criminal will pretend to be a grandchild that is in trouble and needs money. It goes something like this:

Criminal: "Grandma, I'm in trouble and need your help"

Grandma: "Who is this?"

Criminal: "Grandma, it's me"

Grandma: "Johnny, is that you?"

Criminal: "Yes, Grandma. I'm in trouble and need money."

Grandma: "What about your parents? Can't they help you?"

Criminal: "No, Grandma, I don't want them to know. Please, I need your help."

Grandma: "What can I do?"

Criminal: "I need you to send me $3000."

Grandma: "Johnny, that is a lot of money. What kind of trouble are you in?"

Criminal: "The bad kind. Grandma, please!"

Grandma: "Okay"

Many times these calls will come in the middle of the night to catch the victim off guard. If the criminal really wants to be prepared he just needs to turn to the Internet. There he will find family trees, family web pages and more. Thanks to the family tree applications on social networking sites he now has a name to use. If the grandson has posted about his upcoming trip to Mexico, even better. Now he has a name to use and a reason for needing the money. Nothing like scaring Grandma with the "I'm in a Mexican jail and need money" bit to get her to send money.

Bottom line: ask specific questions that only the relative supposedly calling would know. Tell them you will be happy to mail a check and ask where you should send it. If they demand it be wired immediately or for a credit card then ask them for the direct number to the jail, business, or whatever, so you can call them directly. If you don't want to take the chance that it might be a **real** emergency, use another phone to call a second relative for confirmation while this one is on hold. Besides, if the grandson was in trouble, don't you think his parents would want to know?

Solutions

- Ask questions which only the relative would know the answers.
- Contact other family members.
- Do not give out sensitive information. If it is your relative he/she should already know the basics.
- Ask a lot of questions. The more questions you ask the more annoyed the criminal will become and hang up.
- Have a secret code word within your family to use in case of emergency calls.

Garbology

Garbology is a fancy word for dumpster diving. Yes, that is right, digging through the trash. This has been a technique used by criminals through the ages and still, today, provides a treasure trove of information. What is in YOUR garbage? Did you throw away your credit card statement? How about your prescription bottles? Or perhaps it was that pre-approved credit card application? All of these have your sensitive information.

Garbology may very well be a violation of a county ordinance but criminals do not care about breaking the law.

If you don't already own a shredder go out and buy one today. The smaller the cut the better. Confetti cut is much better then crosscut because the shredded pieces are smaller. But don't think that will take care of everything. For around $300, you can buy software online that will reassemble crosscut shredding. That's right - reassemble. Like I said before, if a criminal wants it bad enough he will find a way to get it. There are even companies that make money by reassembling shredded paper.

Paper items are not your only concern. Think before you put your old computer, printer, copy machine, fax machine, or other device curbside. If it has a memory, everything that it created, printed, or copied is stored on the memory. This includes your tax returns.

But don't fret; here are a few simple solutions to reduce your risk:

Solutions

- Shred - shred - shred; this includes ANYTHING with your name on it.
- Don't forget to shred handwritten notes that may contain sensitive information.
- Scrape the label off of your prescription bottle or at a very least,

cross out your information with a black pen.

- Do not put a bag of only shredded papers in your trash. Mix it with your other garbage or pour coffee or water on it. Anything to make it less appealing to criminals.
- Use the shredding in the bottom of your cat litter box. A criminal would have to *really* want your information to go through that!
- Remove the memory from any device before disposing.
- Do not leave any device with a memory unattended curbside.
- Contact your local recycling department to see if they will accept electronic devices for shredding and/or destruction.
- Pay a mobile shredding company to come to your residence. Then you can watch as your papers and devices are destroyed.

Technology

Technology has made our lives easier. Today you can communicate with people from all over the world at any time of day, from anywhere. You can monitor the temperature of your refrigerator from your phone (personally I have not figured out why that would be necessary), you can start your car from your phone, or you can reconnect with high school friends thorough Internet social networking sites. Yes, technology is great. However, it has also made it easier for identity thieves to access your information.

While this section is quite lengthy, please keep in mind that this is not an inclusive list. Technology is constantly evolving. As each new bit of technology is created to make our lives easier, criminals are finding ways to exploit the same technology to steal your money and steal your identity. Please check my website, www.YourPublicIdentity.com, for updates on the types of technology and the techniques used by criminals to steal your information.

Malware

Malware is software that is created with malicious intent and is installed without the owner's informed consent. Examples of malware are viruses, spyware and trojans. Please note these are only a small representation of the types of malware.

Virus

Viruses can do more harm then simply shut down your computer. Viruses can have your computer send out spear phising e-mails (see below), and they can also give the creator, the criminal, complete access to your computer and everything on it. It can also allow the creator to remotely take control of your computer.

Spyware

Spyware is just as the name implies. It is malware that, once installed on a computer, collects bits of information over a period of time, without the owner's consent. Examples of the information collected could be websites visited, Internet usage, Internet buying habits, or passwords typed.

Keyloggers are a type of spyware. Keyloggers allow the criminal to monitor the actions of the computer user. Basically it logs any key stroke, what is typed, and more. It will record e-mails, passwords, web activity, etc. Keyloggers are also used by parents to monitor the Internet activity of minor children. As a side note, keyloggers alone are not effective at protecting a minor on the Internet. Often kids are too smart for these and can figure out how to work around them, or they will just use a computer at a friend's home, the library or on their cell phone. It is best to have an honest conversation with your kids about the dangers of the Internet and let them use the computer at home. Create rules regarding what sites and procedures you do and do not approve, and encourage your kids to talk openly with you when an error in judgment has been made. If you need help, visit my website, www.YourPublicIdentity.com, and click on "Internet Safety Video."

Trojan

A Trojan, also know has a Trojan horse, is malware that is disguised as legitimate software. An example would be when you click on a website and see a pop-up message saying your computer has a virus. The message further states that if you download the free program your computer will be cleaned of the virus. If you click to download the program, you are actually downloading a virus onto your computer. Similar trojans are designed to appear as a pop-up message from your anti-virus program saying a virus has been found. Another technique is offer a free download of an expensive, popular software program.

Recently the FBI cracked a "sextortion" case where a man, through social networking and e-mail, was able to remotely install a Trojan, through a link in an e-mail, onto the computers of teenage girls that he met on a social networking site. This allowed him to activate the computer's webcam without their knowledge. These girls had their computers in their bedroom, and the criminal would activate the webcam while the girl was dressing and undressing, and record the video. Then he used the images from the videos to extort pornographic images of the girls by telling them that if they did not send him nude photos he would notify their parents. The girls gave in because they were afraid of getting into trouble because they had allowed the virus to be installed (unwittingly through the e-mail link) onto the parents computer.

Solutions

- Never click on links in unsolicited e-mails.
- Only download from trusted websites.
- Use anti-virus and spyware blocking programs.
- Use a firewall on your computer.
- Use a pop-up blocker.
- Do not click on pop-ups unless you initiated the pop-up.
- Learn about the dangers of Internet usage.
- Talk to your kids about the dangers of the Internet.
- Talk to your kids about "sextortion."

E-mail Scams

Often I am asked," How do they get my e-mail address?" The answer is simple virus or forwarding. Once a machine is infected with a virus, it then uses the infected machine to send e-mails, with a link that installs the virus, to every contact or e-mail address, on the machine. Another way is through forwarded jokes, urban myths and the sort. You know the ones, "send this back to me if you are my friend" or, "if you don't send this to three people in the next three minutes bad things will happen." Basically these are modern chain letters with a twist. The twist is that they were created to harvest e-mail addresses. Every time the message is forwarded, a blind copy (bcc) is sent to the creator. Once received, all of the "sent to" e-mail addresses are captured for spam and phishing e-mails.

Phishing

Phishing (pronounced "fishing"), is an e-mail disguised to appear to be from a legitimate business or organization. The goals of phishing are to either obtain your personal identifying information such as your SSN, date of birth, or bank account information; or to install software onto your computer giving criminals access to everything on the computer. In the phishing e-mail, a link is provided. Once clicked it will take you to a phony website, designed to look like a legitimate website, and you'll be asked for your personal information. If you are not asked for information, then, typically, the link was to install malware onto your computer.

Spear Phishing

Spear Phishing is an e-mail disguised to appear to be from someone you know, a friend, family member, or colleague. The goals are the same, to get your personal information or to install malware. If you are using a work computer then there is a greater risk for exploitation once the malware is installed on the company network.

Smishing

Smishing is similar to phishing through SMS text messaging. Identity thieves set up an automatic dialing system to send text messages with messages such as "There's a problem with your account" or, "Your ATM card needs to be reactivated." A toll free number is listed and when called, the criminals will proceed to ask for your personal identifying information. If you use a Smartphone (iPhone, Blackberry, or any phone that lets you access the Internet) to call the phone number, malicious software could be uploaded to your phone giving—criminals access to anything on the phone. Remember, Smartphones are just mini versions of computers and they too are susceptible to viruses and other malware.

Vishing

Vishing uses the same technique as Smishing except instead of a text message you receive an phone call or voice mail message.

Solutions

- Never click on a link in an unsolicited e-mail.
- When in doubt, pick up the phone and call the sender to verify.
- Use a spam block to block unsolicited e-mail.
- Do not forward chain letters.
- Ask friends and colleagues to not send you chain letters.
- Educate friends and family on the motivation behind chain letters.
- If your gut tells you something is wrong, listen to it. It is usually

right.

War Driving

War driving is when someone gains access to your wireless network without your permission. There is a simple solution for war driving: password protect and encrypt your wireless router. That's it. Couldn't get any easier. If you do not know how to do this you can hire any computer geek, or, at the very least, someone with just basic computer skills, who can help you can do it yourself. You can also call the help desk for the wireless router company.

One of the largest data security breaches in American history utilized war driving. The criminals parked in front of a business, accessed its wireless network, then accessed its computers, uploaded a Trojan and drove away. The Trojan gathered customer credit card information, which was sent to the criminals. It was just that easy. If someone can get on your network, they can get into your computer and your files.

CAUTION: When using wi-fi hot spots, **do not** access sensitive information such as your bank account. Wi-fi hot spots share a wireless network which can allow anyone with a bit of computer knowledge to access your computer and monitor what you are doing online.

Solutions

- Password protect your wireless network.
- Keep you passwords secured.
- If you do allow others temporary access, change your password when they are finished.

Skimmer

This is a small device used to read the information stored on the magnetic strip on the back of credit cards. These devices are used by identity thieves in restaurants, on ATM machines, and on fuel pumps.

A skimmer is placed inside an ATM card reader and is paired with a small camera, covertly attached to the top of the ATM, to view the PIN pad. Bluetooth technology allows the two devices to communicate with each other. War driving or wireless technology allows the criminal to quickly download the stolen information.

Once the stolen information is obtained, the criminals will either sell the data to other criminals, or will use "flash attacks," which are when gangs of criminals use stolen data to create counterfeit debit cards. Those counterfeit debit cards are dispersed to gang members who are instructed to hit hundreds of ATM machines making a small dollar amount withdrawal at each machine - small enough to go undetected by the victim, but add up to tens of thousands of dollars in profit for the criminals.

Solutions

- Look at the device before swiping your credit/debit card.
- Use credit cards, not debit cards, for purchases.
- Monitor your statements for fraudulent charges.
- Remember, criminals will typically charge less than $10 to your card so it is undetected.
- Keep your receipts so you have the details of your transactions.

Bluetooth

Bluetooth technology allows two or more devices to communicate, such as a computer or a cell phone. If you do not password protect your computer or cell phone, any Bluetooth-enable hardware can connect and communicate giving access to sensitive information.

Solutions

- Password protect Bluetooth access.
- Configure your device to notify you of all Bluetooth access requests.

USB Drives

USB drives, also known as flash drives or jump drives, are small handheld devices that allow you to store numerous amounts of data, music or videos. Basically these are portable storage devices. These devices are small enough to fit on a key ring, or can be concealed in a bracelet. One gigabyte (1GB) can hold over 650,000 text pages. That is a ton of information on such a small device. Downloading takes mere seconds. Just simply install the device, click a few buttons to start downloading files, and "Bam!" in a few minutes you are done.

I am not going to explain the "few buttons" as this is not a "how to commit ID theft" book. Criminals have used this simple technique to steal customer data from businesses. Typically, it is an inside job where an employee is offered money in exchange for downloading the information.

If you use a USB device as a back up for your records then you could also be putting yourself at risk. If the USB drive is stolen and it is not encrypted, the information is now available to whomever possess the unit. Basically you have just wrapped up your sensitive files in a nice pretty bow and given it to the criminal.

Solutions

- Password protect your computer.
- Block unnecessary USB ports.
- Password protect sensitive files and folders on your computer and device.
- Password protect your USB device.
- Protect your USB device as you would other sensitive information.

Cell Phones

Cell phones today are mini computers. No longer does a cell phone just make a call. Now you have e-mail, texting, web browsing (Internet surfing), and all of those wonderful apps (short for applications). There is an "app" for just about anything. Some "apps" notify you of a sale as you walk past the store, others allow you to access social networking on the go, and others allow friends and family to locate you through GPS technology. Forget the government being "big brother" - you are willingly allowing the world to monitor your every move through the use of "apps." But that is not the worst of it. Some "apps" are actually trojans. Once installed on your phone the virus will be installed on your computer when you synch them together.

Cell phones also come with a built-in camera and/or video recorder. Now you can take a photo or video of little Johnny at his basketball game or Susie at her dance recital. But cell phones are also being used by criminals to steal your information. As mentioned before, if you have bank or credit card statements lying around, anyone in view of them can copy them just by using the camera on a cell phone.

Cell phones also hold a ton of information. If your accountant e-mailed you a copy of your tax return to your phone, the document is stored on the phone. If your phone is lost or stolen, the criminal now has the document bearing your name, address, date of birth and social security number. Many people also keep passwords stored in an app on their phone. If it is not password protected, the criminal now has access to your passwords. Basically, they have now found the "keys to the kingdom," such as your online bank account password.

Solutions

- Password protect your cell phone.
- Be selective when choosing apps.
- Read the Terms of Service and Privacy Policy for the app before using or purchasing.
- Back up the information on your cell phone regularly.
- Purchase software to destroy the data on a Smartphone if stolen or lost.
- Consider the trade off between convenience and loss of privacy.

Spoofing

Spoofing is when a criminal manipulates caller ID so it appears to be a call from a legitimate company. For example, you receive a call from someone at ABC bank notifying you that your account has been suspended. Caller ID shows "ABC Bank" so you provide them with the information requested, and now the criminal has your information. Caller ID spoofing is very easy to do, you just sign up online, and it is very inexpensive. A perfect combination for criminals.

Solutions

- Just because it says a name on caller ID does not mean that it is the ID of the caller.
- When in doubt, call the company at the phone listed online, in the phone book or in directory assistance.
- Never give out sensitive information on calls you did not initiate.

RFID

RFID, or Radio Frequency IDentification, consists of a small computer chip and an antenna. These chips hold the same information as the magnetic strip on the back of a credit card. They must be scanned by an RFID reader just as a regular credit card must be scanned before making a purchase. A criminal, using equipment that cost less than $200, can walk past you and skim your credit card information right out of your purse or wallet. The RFID emits a chirp, an invisible radio wave, detected by the RFID reader. Fortunately, many of us carry multiple credit cards so the chirping from multiple cards could become muddled. While this risk is limited, it is still a risk that you are unable to control, unless of course, you decide to only carry cash.

So how do you know if your credit card has been RFID? Call your credit card company and ask them if it is RFID-enabled. Another tip-off is a credit card that is referred to as "easy pay." Credit card companies know that the majority of American would object to receiving a RFID-enabled card so they trick you by selling the benefits such as easy pay.

Okay, now I'm going to get a little Big Brother-ish. There are people in the technology world who believe RFID can be used to track you. By placing RFID readers in numerous locations, every time you walk by a reader, the time and date is logged by the reader. The information that is read is whatever information has been placed on the RFID chip. It could be your name, address and credit card number, or a product ID number. Currently RFID technology is used in the retail industry to prevent and detect shoplifting. RFID's are small and can easily be sewn into a hem, sandwiched between cardboard, or incorporated into plastic packaging. Each time you enter or exit a store with an RFID enabled product, the RFID reader is taking notes. Retailers could use this information to learn buying habits. The same technology could be used to track your whereabouts as you enter and exit stores with RFID readers. Like I said, Big Brother-ish.

Solutions

- Skip convenience and stick to privacy.
- Opt out of RFID credit cards.
- Call your credit card company and ask if your credit card is RFID enabled.
- Monitor your credit card statements for fraudulent activity.

Internet

The Internet provides criminals easy access to your personal identifying information. It has also turned your private identity public. How? A few of these items were already covered in the Technology section, such as phishing and malware. Now, let's take a closer look at the Internet and how your data is exposed.

Social Networking

For those of you that have never heard of social networking, let me take a moment to explain what it is. Social networking sites allow you to "friend" someone, a friend, a relative, a colleague, etc, for the purpose of keeping up to date with each other's activities; basically to keep in touch. A few examples of these sites would be Facebook, Friendster, or LinkedIn. Some are designed for personal relationships (think Facebook), and others are designed for professional relationships (such as LinkedIn). You can also make connections, which allow you to become "friends" with someone you do not know but want to know. There are also apps for games, surveys, or sharing interest in a cause.

Social networking is interesting in the aspect that people will post information that they would never say out loud or post on a billboard on the side of the highway. But in essence, that is exactly what they are doing. For some reason people seem to think that social networking sites are private. This is a HUGE misconception. Nothing on the Internet is private. Let me say this again, NOTHING ON THE INTERNET IS PRIVATE. Even if you set your profile to "private" it is **still** not private. Quite often in my investigations, I am able to access information from a private site without hacking or through any illegal activity. Criminals on the other hand, have no problem breaking laws and will hack or use other illegal tactics to get your information.

Your Profile

Your profile typically consists of your name, city and state, date of birth, employer, hobbies, marital status, and so on. This is all useful information to a criminal. A criminal can use this information to assume your identity and scam your friends and family.

Solutions

- Hide your date of birth.
- Limit the information on your profile.
- Set your profile as "private".
- Be generic on your profile.

Family Trees

If you use a family tree on your profile, you have now just given a criminal a list of names to use in the phone scam posing as a relative in trouble (mentioned earlier). Or you have now just given the criminal your mother's maiden name, a common security questions.

Solutions

- Do not use family trees on your social networking profile.

Apps

Apps sound like fun and useful tools, however they pose a security risk. Before you can activate an app you must click that you are allowing a third party access to your profile information and all of your friend's information. Facebook, in early 2010, reached a settlement in a class action lawsuit from its "Beacon" program, which tracked the purchases and video rentals of its members. One member's profile revealed a post about a recent diamond ring purchase from an online retailer after he made the purchase. He did not post the information, but the information was posted automatically after his purchase. This post was then read by all of his friends - including his wife. Facebook denied the charges.

Another app shared member profile information, and the member's friend's profile information, to dozens of Internet tracking and advertising companies. This app was not developed by the social networking site but by a third party, which the app users agreed to provide access to their profile information and friend's information.

Solutions

- Read and understand the Terms of Service agreements.
- Know what information and access you are giving companies.
- Do not accept or participate in apps.
- Ask friends and family not to send you app requests.

Posts

Posts are information you write into your profile to share with your friends. Some people post about having their morning cup of coffee. Others post the progress of their morning run, map and all. Still others post their current location using an app and their cell phone. Or they post information about their upcoming vacation. All of these are, in my mind, too much information. Do I really need to know that you had your morning coffee? No. But if I was a criminal I would definitely want the other information.

For a moment, I am going to veer away from identity theft and talk about other potentially dangerous crimes. If I know that every morning at 5:00 AM you head out for your morning run and you have provided me a map of where you run, don't you think it will be easy for me to know exactly where you will be tomorrow so I can kidnap you or break into your home? Same for the GPS tracking. If I am a stalker, I know exactly where you are. If am robbing your home, I know exactly how much time I have before you will return home from shopping - or better yet, your vacation. I am not making this stuff up, folks. There have been warnings from law enforcement about posting upcoming vacation details on social networking sites. You might as well put a sign in your yard that says, "Gone on vacation, criminals are invited to take what they want while I'm gone."

Solutions

- If you wouldn't post it on a billboard, don't post it online.
- Do not post anything that is private.
- Remember, social networking sites are not a digital diary.

- Do not post when you will be gone for an extended period of time, or that you are out of town.
- Do not post your daily routine.
- Do not allow GPS tracking of your location from your phone.

Online Friends

Social networking is not an online popularity contest. You do not have to be friends with everyone. Be selective about who you accept a friends. If you don't know the person, reject the friend request. If the girls that were victims in the "sextortion" case mentioned previously would have been taught this, they may not have become victims.

Also, remember that just because someone says they are a friend does not mean they are who they claim to be. I refer to this as "fake facing" - when someone steals your identity to create a social networking profile. This happens more often than you think. If you don't have a social networking profile, check the site to see if one with your name is already there. One client called saying she was receiving death threats because someone had 'faked faced' her and was making slanderous and derogatory posts about others. Another client's ex-girlfriend hacked into his profile. The ex-girlfriend, posing as him, was contacting his friends and clients through the social networking site.

Solutions

- Only friend people you know.
- Don't take every post at face value.
- When in doubt, call the person on the telephone.
- Check to see if you have a profile you did not create.

Tweeting and Blogging

Tweeting and blogging are other ways private information becomes public. Just as with posting on social networking sites, you must remember that everything you tweet, a post on Twitter, or a blog is public information. In fact, the Library of Congress is now archiving every tweet on Twitter. That is right. If you post it, it will be archived forever for anyone to read.

Blogs are much longer than tweets. Tweets are limited to 140 characters where blogs are unlimited. Blogs are a great way to share useful information. I have a blog for my investigation company, www..MarconeInvestigations.com/blog, where I post information on frauds and scams. But some people use their blog as an online diary. Just as in in social networking posts, they will share the details of their life. This information is available for anyone to view.

These can also be a great source for you to search for a breach of your information. We will discuss that later in the book.

Solutions

- Keep it simple.
- Filter your posts.
- Less is best when it comes to personal information.

File Sharing and the Cloud

File sharing sites do exactly as the name implies. However, if you are not careful, you could end up sharing every file on your computer. When setting up an account, make sure you read and understand the Terms of Service Agreement and Privacy Policy. You also want to pay careful attention to the settings when choosing which files to share. If you choose "share all" then that is what will happen - anyone with an account can access all of your computer files including your tax return.

Cloud computing is a form of file sharing. Clouds are virtual storage devices. They allow you to store all of your files on a server that is not in your home or at your work. This allows for you to save tons of information without overloading your computer. However, storing information in the cloud is risky. Anytime information is floating in cyberspace it is vulnerable to a breach, which could occur while you are accessing your information or while information is stored on the offsite server. Some cloud companies offer more security than others but you will pay for the extra security.

Solutions

- Pay attention to what files you allow access to when file sharing.
- Read the Terms of Service Agreement and Privacy Policy.
- Know how your information is being protected.
- Know who has access to your information.
- Encrypt your folders and/or files for an extra layer of protection.
- Purchase an external hard drive to store excess data. Encrypt the external hard drive for protection.

Public Records

Did you know that in a as little as five minutes, I can find out if you own your home, how much you paid for it, if you have a mortgage, and get a diagram of your residence? I, and anyone with a computer, can do all of this by using online public records. Your local Clerk of Courts uploads your information to the Internet. Now, some of these sites require payment, others require you to create an account, and still others are not yet online. These are merely minor setbacks for a criminal. They can easily overcome these and get your information. I have even found older documents online that have SSN's, dates of birth and account information. By law, this information is supposed to be redacted, thanks to human error, a few are missed. If the information is not yet online, I can simply visit the local clerk's office and ask to see the file. Again, I have found personal financial statements, SSN, dates of birth and account information in these files.

There are also data mining sites that gather the information found online and provide them to anyone that wants them for a small fee. How do they do it? They use a bot. Think of a bot as a dog that is let loose to retrieve a ball. In the case of a bot, data is the ball. The bot brings back the data where it is sorted and matched by specific criteria. This is all automated and is done in seconds. Another example of a bot is a Google search. You tell it what you want and it retrieves the information.

Recently a father was searching his child's name online and came across his own personal information and that of his child. It turns out a school employee mistakenly uploaded a file of all student and parent information to the Internet instead of the school's intranet. The information listed everything about his child – including his name and SSN.

Solutions

- Search the Internet for your public identity.
- Never search by your SSN.
- Know what information is in your public records.
- Review your public records and request a redaction of sensitive information such as SSN.
- Search engines only search the web surface. You need to also search the deep web. (I will show you how later in this book)

WORKSHEET

The next few pages contain a worksheet for you to use while reading this section. The worksheet lists the most common ways you could be making your private identity public. While reading this section, when you come across an item that you are doing, or not doing, place a checkmark in the appropriate box. Each item has three options: not currently doing, needs improvement, and doing consistently. Be honest with yourself.

For items that you originally check as "not currently doing" , make the changes to reduce your risk then check "needs improvement". Once the changes made become part of your routine, check "doing consistently".

You are not expected to make all of the changes right away. Start with the one or two a day and work your way through the remainder of the list. I have been told it takes thirty days to change a habit.

HOW TO AVOID BECOMING A VICTIM

*   Not currently doing
**   Needs improvement
***   Doing consistently

Purse/Wallet

	*	**	***
photocopied items			
only carry essentials			
low credit limit			
no SSN card			
no PIN printed			
never leave unattended			
signed credit cards			

Unlocked Mailbox

	*	**	***
incoming mail			
outgoing mail			

Service Providers/Guests

	*	**	***
sensitive info locked/hidden			
file cabinet key hidden			
file cabinet locked			
request criminal backgrounds			

Home Computers   *   **   ***

	*	**	***
password protected			
encrypted wireless network			
screen saver with password			

Pretexting   *   **   ***

	*	**	***
never give sensitive information			
no donations by phone			
no phone surveys			
prizes are free			
don't hire by solicitation only			
grants are not for individuals			
you can't win without an entry			
ask a lot of questions			
have a secret family code word			
contact family members			

Garbology   *   **   ***

	*	**	***
shred, shred, shred			
confetti shredder			
pour liquid on shredded paper			
no prescription labels			
remove device memory			

Technology   *   **   ***

	*	**	***
use anti-virus software			
use firewall			
use spam blockers			
use pop-up blockers			
unsolicited email links			
do not click pop-ups			
family internet rules			
talk to kids about internet			
when in doubt, call			
do not forward chain letters			
look before swipe card			
monitor statements			
password on Bluetooth			
encrypt sensitive files			
encrypt USB devices			
password on cell phone			
be selective with apps			
read TOS agreements			
back up cell phone data			
ask if RFID credit card			
cancel RFID credit cards			

Internet

	*	**	***
private profile			
hidden date of birth			
no family tree			
social networking apps			
no GPS tracking			
no digital diary			
no vacation announcement			
friend only friends			
find your profile			
when in doubt, call			
keep it simple			
read TOS agreements			
ask questions			
encrypt files			
do not file share everything			
search public records			
search the deep web			

NOTES:

GET PROACTIVE

I am sure that after reading the last section you are thinking that there is no hope. You may feel a bit scared, perhaps a bit paranoid as well. You are not alone. You need to get scared before you will start to take action to reduce your risk. Keep going, you will be glad you did.

Before reading this section make sure you completed the "How To Become a Victim" worksheet. This will help you focus on the areas where your information is at the greatest risk of exposure.

Now that you know how criminals steal your information, it is time to learn how to reduce your risk. This section will dig deeper into tips, techniques and resources to reduce your risk of becoming an identity theft victim.

Please keep in mind that you will need to use these tips, techniques and resources multiple times. Monitoring your information is a long-term commitment. But that commitment can become less of a burden by using the worksheets at the end of the section.

How To Monitor Your Identity

As stated earlier in this book, your private information is already out. It is your responsibility to know where it is, who has access to it, and how is it being used. Here are a few tools to use to check your identity:

Google Alerts

Google Alerts are bots you create to search the Internet for specific information, such as your name. To create a Google Alert visit www.google.com/alerts. Enter the information you want to search into the "search terms" box. You can test your search parameters by clicking on "Preview results." If you enter your search terms surrounded by quotes (example: "Carrie Kerskie"), you will get any results with the words Carrie and Kerskie directly next to each other. If you have a common name, use your first and last name, the "+" sign, then city and state.

Next, choose the type of data you want Google to search. I recommend you select "Everything" for maximum results. You can even choose how frequently you will receive the search results from Google. At a minimum, select "Everyday." After that, you will need to select the volume of results. Do you want all results or only the best results? Depending on your name you may need to test these settings. If the volume of results is extremely large, change to only the best results.

Finally, you must enter your email address. The search results will be sent to the email address entered into this section. Then, click "Create Alert" and you are done. It is just that simple. You can also create alerts for your children, your business and anything else you want to monitor online.

www.PIPL.com

This is a great resource for deep web searches. Visit www.pipl.com and enter the information based on the tabs: Name, Email, Username and Phone. You can also search by business name but this feature is still in beta testing and may not be as accurate. If you have a common name, you will find information that is not related to you. This is normal, since it is using bots to search deep web. Remember, bots are like a dog retrieving a ball. It might not bring back the same ball you threw, but it will bring back a ball.

County Clerk of Courts

The easiest way to find the Clerk of Courts for your County is to do an online search. Put the name of the county you live in, followed by "Clerk of Courts" in quotation marks and then search. Not all counties are online so make sure you are not at a generic paid site, but are at the actual county website. Once on the website, look for "online searching" or "online services." These typically list how you can search for records online. The most accurate way to search is by visiting your local Clerk of Courts office. County workers will either let you search on a public computer or they will search the records for you. Remember, your goal is to know what information is available to other people besides you.

County Property Appraiser

Just as with the Clerk of Courts, you will need to first discover if property records are available online in your county. If they are, how can they be searched? By owner's name, by property address or by other information? Once searched, view the results. Is there any sensitive information available to the general public? You can also visit your local Property Appraiser's office and ask what information is available to you for review and what information is available to the general public.

Division of Motor Vehicles

Contact your state DMV and request a full history of your driving record. There will be a fee associated with the request, so ask in advance how much it will cost. You will have to show proof of identification before the record will be released to you.

State Department of Law Enforcement

A quick online search using the name of your state and "department of law enforcement" or "state police" should point you in the right direction. You can also search "how to get a Florida (or state where you live) criminal records report?" As with the other searches, make sure you are on the state's official website and not a generic paid website. You will be charged a fee and may also be asked to provide fingerprints or proof of ID.

County Sheriff's Office

The method is similar for the state criminal records check. First, find the website. Then, request a background check based on their requirements. If you prefer to contact them by phone, ask to speak to the Records Department.

www.AnnualCreditReport.com

The website to request free copies of your credit reports is www.annualcreditreport.com. This is the ONLY website endorsed by the Federal Trade Commission and is the ONLY true, free website. When you attempt an online request at one of the credit bureau's websites you are redirected to www.annualcreditreport.com. It does take sometime to get through all of the questions since you're identity is being validated to protect you. Be sure to have account numbers handy and don't try to complete the website while you are multitasking.

If you should have any difficulty in locating any of the above websites you can log onto the Member's Only page of my website, www.YourPublicIdentity.com, to request a link. You will need to create a free account by entering your name and email address along with the code *ypisckg*. I will also update the site with new search tools as they are discovered.

Read Your Statements

Do you reconcile your statements every month? Come on, be honest. If so, you are ahead of the game. This is one of the easiest ways to reduce your risk and detect if your information has been exposed.

Each month, you receive a statement for your bank account, credit card, savings account, mortgage and any other account involving credit or money. These statements show you the activity in your account for a period of time, either monthly, quarterly, or yearly. It is your responsibility to check them for accuracy.

Your statement will arrive at the same time each month, give or take a few days. If you do not receive a statement when expected, contact the business. This could be a sign that someone has stolen your mail. Using the excuse, "but I didn't receive a statement" does not offer you any protection. It is your responsibility to contact the business when you have not received your statement.

Look over your statement with a fine tooth comb - line by line, item by item. If there is *anything* that you do not recognize then make a call. Either call the company where the item was purchased or call the bank or credit card for additional information to help you reconcile, it is a good idea to keep all receipts in a folder and match them to your statement each month. Once they have been verified you can shred the receipts. Talk to your accountant about what receipts you need to save to assist with your tax return.

If a discrepancy is noted, you are required to notify the business (bank or credit card company) within their required period of time, typically 60 days. The required time period can be found in your agreement when you first opened the account, printed on your statement, or you can contact the business. It is important that you know how many days you have to report a discrepancy and each company's reporting procedures. If you do not report within the guidelines then you increase your liability. It is always best to notify in writing. This gives you documentation of your contact and puts the company on alert. A phone call can be ignored or forgotten.

Make sure to keep a log of the discrepancy, when it was

detected, when you notified the business and when it was corrected. You also want to write down the date, time and contact person for each and every telephone conversation. This helped me when a company tried to deny my request. I knew they recorded all conversations. I told them the date and time of my call and suggested they pull the recorded calls from that date. They did, apologized for their oversight and fixed the error. To aid you in this process you can use the worksheet found in the Resource section of this book. You also want to keep all correspondence with the business. This will protect you in the event the same item appears at a later date.

Lock It Up

Locking up sensitive information seems like a simple thing to do. So then why do I find so many keys sitting in file cabinet locks when I do an information security audit? Or better yet, I find the cabinet locked but the key sitting on top of the cabinet. This is not rocket science, folks. Lock it up and hid the key. But it is much more then just file cabinets. Here are the most common mistakes I observe when it comes to information security:

Sensitive Documents

As I mentioned before, do not leave your sensitive documents lying around your home. When you are not reconciling them, keep them locked in a file cabinet. Purchase the best you can afford. There are two drawer locking units that cost around $40. They are not the best or most secure, but they provide an extra layer of protection. It is much easier to notice a damaged or stolen file cabinet than it is to notice a stolen piece of paper.

Now that you have spent the money on a file cabinet, make sure you use it correctly. Keep it locked unless you are putting something away or taking something out. This way if someone were to break into your home you would not have to worry about them now stealing your identity on top of stealing your valuables. After you have locked it, place the key in a well hidden place. The most obvious places, and I have found keys here, are in the cabinet key lock, on top of the cabinet, taped to the side of the cabinet, in a desk drawer next to the cabinet, or on a key rack. If your file cabinet does not have a lock, then purchase a lock unit at your local hardware store. They are easy to install. If you have lost the keys to your file cabinet you can order replacements online. All you need is the maker of the cabinet and the number on the locking unit. In the past, I have purchased replacement keys from www.EasyKeys.com. A simple Internet search will reveal many sources for replacement keys.

Mail

Stealing mail is one of the oldest crimes around. It is simple, takes little to no skill, and can be done anywhere there are mailboxes. If you are placing your payment to the credit card company in an unlocked mailbox - it is fair game. Yes, it is a federal offense to steal from a mailbox but these are criminals. They don't typically follow the laws.

You have two choices: get a USPS approved locking mailbox or get a post office box. USPS approved mailboxes can be purchased online or at major home repair stores (such as Lowes or Home Depot).

Data Storage Devices

Data storage devices are used to store data. These include, but are not limited to, CD's, hard drives, portable USB drives, DVD's, laptops, notebooks, netbooks, and cell phones. These devices are easy targets for criminals wanting to get your information. All they have to do is take the device, put it in another computer and open the file(s).

For laptops, notebooks or netbooks, they just need to power it up.

For other devices lock them in a file cabinet or lockbox when not in use. If you must carry these with you, it is best to encrypt the device or each individual file. The level of encryption will be based on the type of information stored on the device.

For greater protection you could encrypt the file and also encrypt the device. Opening the device would require a password and so would the files. This is a double layer of protection but may not be practical for everyday use. Just remember, the more sensitive the information, the more layers of protection that are warranted. If you do not know how to encrypt a file, you can search the Internet for instructions. Often times you can right mouse click on the folder or file name, click properties and from the 'advanced' button choose encryption. There are also software programs you can download or purchase to encrypt a device. Before purchasing make sure to search for product reviews from multiple sites.

For laptops, notebooks, and netbooks it is not reasonable to expect you to keep these locked in a file cabinet. But you can take simple steps such as password protecting the computer. When the computer is started, access to files and programs are restricted by a password. This is layer one. You can then encrypt folders and files as needed. This is layer two. In the event your laptop is stolen, you can install software with GPS to track your laptop and a kill switch to wipe the data making it unusable by the criminal. This would be layer three.

You can do the same for your cell phone, depending on the make and model. Smartphones are mini computers and should be treated as such. Password protect your cell phone. It may be inconvenient to have to enter the password all of the time but it will save your data if your phone is stolen. There is also software you can purchase that will track your phone, GPS, or remotely delete the data in the event it is stolen or lost. You can ask your cell phone carrier for recommendations, or a simple Internet search for "disable stolen cell phone" will list a few. Again, just make sure you also search for reviews of the software before purchasing.

Cyber Safety

As discussed earlier in this book, there are dangers lurking on the Internet. If you are not careful you personally could contribute to making your private identity public. There are a few simple rules I created to help you proceed with caution while using the Internet.

Stop-Think-Click

Step One - Stop

- Before doing anything on the Internet, stop, and take a moment to pause before reacting. This applies to posting, replying to e-mails, buying online and downloading.

Step Two - Think

- Ask yourself these questions:
- Who is the originating source? Is it legitimate or spear phishing?
- Who am I sending it to? Did you hit reply or reply all?
- What will happen if I reply, post or click?
- What will happen if I do nothing?
- Where will this information go? Who will have access to it?
- Do I have to do this now or can it wait?
- How will this affect me or others? Now or in the future?

Step Three - Click
- Once you are satisfied with your answers, proceed to click.

Think Outside the Web

It is easy to get caught up in the virtual world of the Internet. But, you must always remember that what you do online can and will effect your real life. If you are posting about your upcoming vacation you are also telling thieves to "come and get it".

When in doubt, pick up the telephone and call the person or business. If you have received a suspicious e-mail or just read a slanderous post about you, before you take action online, contact the sender or poster and verify the information. You just may learn that your call is the first the person had heard about it.

Important conversations should always be conducted face-to-face. When speaking to someone in the virtual world, you have no way of verifying their identity. By conversing face-to-face you can confirm their identity and observed social cues such as their facial expression and body language. You can also verify if you are conversing with a fifty-five-year old man or your sixteen-year-old granddaughter.

You can also avoid the common mistake of misinterpretation. When conversing online, you can only read letters on a screen. There is no emotion, no feedback. Have you ever received an e-mail from someone and thought they were either mad at your or were being rude, only later to find that they were not? Or while typing they asked to you to do something when they meant to ask you *not* to do something but forgot to type the word "not?" If you are conversing online, don't take everything at face value. Pick up the phone and talk to the person.

Self Monitoring

It is your responsibility to know what information about you is already floating around in cyberspace. But first you need to know where to look. If you can't find your information, how can you protect it?

This information was previously mentioned in this book, but it's worth reiterating. Search the following site to check up on yourself.

- ➤ Google Alerts
- ➤ PIPL
- ➤ Clerk of Court
- ➤ Property Appraiser
- ➤ Division of Motor Vehicles
- ➤ State Department of Law Enforcement
- ➤ County Sheriff's Office
- ➤ Annual Credit Report

Remember, if you can't find your information, how can you protect it? So start searching.

Opt Out

Did you know that you can opt out of receiving nearly all of the sales solicitations you are bombarded with every day? You just need to know how to do it.

To opt out of pre-approved credit card offers call

1-888-5-OPT-OUT (567-8688)

To opt out of receiving any commercial mail from many national companies for five years, use the Direct Marketing Association's (DMA) Mail Preference Service. There is a $1 fee to register your name onto the "delete" file that is made available to direct-mail marketers. Visit www.DMAChoice.org to register. Please note that this will *not* prevent you from receiving mail from marketers that do not use DMA's Preference Service.

It is not as easy to opt out of other types of solicitations. Most of the companies you do business with either share your contact information (name and address) or make money from selling your contact information to other companies. Then these companies send you offers for their products or services. Some companies even track your buying habits, frequency and the products you use, and share or sell these to other companies. This is all done with your permission. Right now you are probably saying, "But I never gave them permission!" If you signed up for a rewards program you did. These programs are disguised to make you think you are getting special privileges and maybe even save you a bit of money. But the intended purpose is to track your buying habits and increase revenue for the company offering the program.

You can opt out by not signing up for these programs in the first place. Yes, you will lose the coupon or promotion promised, but you will be reducing your public identity.

Other companies have data sharing language in the fine print of their agreements when you open an account. Think of credit card companies and banks. In the multi-page fine print of pamphlet you receive when you open an account is information about how the company shares your information. Federal law now requires that companies also tell you how to opt out of data sharing. Many times it is a simple as a phone call. Other times, you must submit the request in writing. Either way, opt out. If you cannot find the agreement pamphlet, contact the company and ask out to opt out. These companies do not want to you to opt out and will make it difficult for you to find this information on their website. Ask them to send you the instructions in writing. Then document when you contacted them (including date and time) to opt out.

By opting out, your information will no longer be allowed to be shared by the company, greatly reducing the amount of received sales solicitations. It will reduce your ever increasing public identity.

If you want to opt out of additional credit accounts, you can place a security freeze (also known as a credit freeze), on your credit report. This freeze will restrict anyone from obtaining a copy of your credit history. Depending on your state, a small fee may be charged, around $10, unless you are a victim of identity theft. If you are an ID theft victim you must provide a copy of the police report, an ID theft affidavit and other documents to have the fee waived. You will need to contact each credit bureau directly to request the security freeze.

A credit freeze does NOT offer you any protection from fraud on your current accounts and does NOT guarantee new accounts will be established in your name. It will only notify you when a copy of your credit history is requested. If you are actively using your credit, buying a home or car, do not put a security freeze on your credit history because this will delay or prevent you from obtaining the loan. It is best to wait until your loan is approved and established before initiating a security freeze.

In the event you want to remove the security freeze, each credit bureau will again charge you small fee. Each time you initiate and remove a security freeze you will incur that fee.

WORKSHEET

The next few pages contain a worksheet for you to use while reading this section. The worksheet lists simple tools and techniques to use to reduce your risk of identity theft. While reading this section, when you come across an item that you are doing, or not doing, place a checkmark in the appropriate box. Each item has three options: not currently doing, needs improvement, and doing consistently. Be honest with yourself.

For items that you originally check as "not currently doing" , make the changes to reduce your risk then check "needs improvement". Once the changes made become part of your routine, check "doing consistently".

You are not expected to make all of the changes right away. Start with the one or two a day and work your way through the remainder of the list. As stated earlier in this book, it takes thirty days to change a habit.

GET PROACTIVE WORKSHEET

* Not currently doing
** Needs improvement
*** Doing consistently

Monitor Your ID   *   **   ***   Notes

	*	**	***	Notes
Google Alerts				
PIPL				
Clerk of Courts				
Property Appraiser				
Dept. of Motor Vehicles				
State Law Enforcement				
County Law Enforcement				
AnnualCreditReport.com				

Reconcile Monthly   *   **   ***   Notes

	*	**	***	Notes
Checking				
Savings				
Investments				
Loans				
Credit Card				
Equity Line				

Lock It Up   *   **   ***   Notes

	*	**	***	Notes
Locked file cabinet				
Hidden key				

Mail   *   **   ***   Notes

	*	**	***	Notes
Locked mailbox				
Post office box				

Data Storage Devices   *   **   ***   Notes

Password protect/ Encrypt

	*	**	***	Notes
desktop				
laptop				
netbook				
cell phone				
portable storage devices				

Cyber Safety   *   **   ***   Notes

	*	**	***	Notes
Stop-Think-Click				
Think Outside the Web				
Self Monitoring				

Opt Out   *   **   ***   Notes

	*	**	***	Notes
888-5-OPT-OUT				
DMA				

Technology	*	**	***	Notes
use anti-virus software				
use firewall				
use spam blockers				
use pop-up blockers				
unsolicited email links				
do not click pop-ups				
family internet rules				
talked to kids about internet				
when in doubt, call				
do not forward chain letters				
look before swipe card				
monitor statements				
password on Bluetooth				
encrypt sensitive files				
encrypt USB devices				
password on cell phone				
be selective with apps				
read TOS agreements				
back up cell phone data				
ask if RFID credit card				
cancel RFID credit cards				

Internet	*	**	***	Notes
private profile				
hidden date of birth				
no family tree				
social networking apps				
no GPS tracking				
no digital diary				
no vacation announcement				
friend only friends				
find your profile				
when in doubt, call				
keep it simple				
read TOS agreements				
ask questions				
encrypt files				
do not file share everything				
search public records				
search the deep web				

NOTES:

WARNING SIGNS

If your identity has been compromised, there are warning signs available to you if you know where to look. These warning signs should set off a red flag that you may be a victim of identity theft or fraud.

Statements

As mentioned earlier, your bank or credit card statements can be your best source for financial identity theft detection. By diligently reviewing every transaction on every statement every month you will be able to detect fraudulent activity. If you can monitor your statements online- even better. You will be able to detect the fraud immediately. The sooner you detect the fraud, the sooner you can take action, limiting your exposure and liability.

Another sign of possible fraud is a notification of a change of address request. If you receive this type of letter do not discard it as an error. Contact the business right away. Someone is trying to change your mailing address so you do not receive a statement. By not receiving a statement, you cannot detect the fraudulent activity in your account.

Health insurance Explanation of Benefits (EOB) is another statement that you need to carefully review. Any discrepancies could indicate you have been a victim of medical identity theft. Contact the insurance company and ask for additional information on the claim, such as the contact information (phone number and mailing address) for the healthcare provider that submitted the claim. If you still do not recognize the claim contact the fraud department with your insurance carrier. If you do not have insurance and receive a bill for medical services you did not receive, you need to contact the healthcare provider immediately and report the discrepancy. You may also need to contact law enforcement to file a report. The police may not open an investigation, but you may need the report when attempting to amend your medical record or credit report.

WARNING SIGNS

- Unrecognized transactions
- Changes to your account information.
- Notification of a change of address request.
- EOB for services or treatment you did not receive.
- Receive a statement from a healthcare provider you do not recognize.

Credit Reports

The Fair Credit Reporting Act (FCRA) requires the credit reporting bureaus to provide you with a free copy of your credit report every twelve months. Here is how you can get three free credit reports in twelve months. Every four months obtain a credit report from a different bureau.

Your credit report will help you determine if you have been a victim of financial identity theft. Many identity theft victims never knew they were a victim until they reviewed their credit reports.

There are three credit reporting bureaus: Experian, TransUnion and Equifax. You need to review reports from all three as not all creditors report to all three bureaus. It is not uncommon to see a credit account reflected on one report but not on the other two. Below are the sections of the credit reports by bureau. Please note that your report may contain additional sections, or may not include a section that is listed below. These are listed just as a guideline so you know where to look for possible fraudulent activity.

Experian

1. Applicant Information - Provided

> This section reflects the information submitted to request the credit report. It also lists the report number, which you will need this if there is a discrepancy; and the date of the request.

2. Potentially Negative Items

> Just as the name implies, this section highlights any potentially negative items reflected on your credit report. This area is key as it may be your first detection of identity theft.

3. Public Records

> This section reflects public records from your county Clerk of the Courts. Criminal and/or civil information may be reflected here. If a record is indicated that you do not recognize, contact your county clerk's office for additional information.

4. Credit Items

This is where all of your credit accounts are listed. Typically included are the name, address and phone number of the creditor; status of the account; when the account was opened; credit limit; balance; person(s) responsible for the account; and recent payment information. Account history will list if the account is current or late based on tiered dates, 30 days, 60 days, and so on.

If you detect an account that you do not recognize, contact the credit bureau for additional information. If an account reflects a higher balance or late payments, again, contact the creditor.

5. Accounts in Good Standing

These accounts have a positive status and are viewed favorably by creditors. The account type will also be listed. Types include, but are not limited to, installment, revolving, or mortgage.

6. Request For Your Credit History

This is where recent inquiries into your credit history are listed. There are two types of inquiries: "Request Viewed by Others" and "Request Viewed Only by You."

"Requests Viewed by Others" lists inquiries resulting from a transaction you, such as car loan or transferring an account to a collections account. These inquiries can have an effect on your credit report as they are viewed by creditors when deterring your creditworthiness. Look for inquires from any creditors you are not familiar with and accounts that have been transferred to collections. These are strong indicators of possible fraud - that is, as long as you yourself have not caused the account to have been transferred to collections.

"Requests Viewed Only by You" lists inquiries resulting from transactions you may not have initiated, but that are allowed under FCRA, such as pre-approved offers, employment, or monitoring of your account (credit monitoring). These have no impact on your credit score and are not revealed to other creditors. It is normal to see inquiries from unknown creditors.

If you opt-out, this will greatly reduce the number of unknown creditors reflected in this section.

7. Personal Information

This is personal information that has been reported to Experian by you, creditors or other sources. It may include, address information (current and/or previous), SSN, year of birth, co-applicant (spouse), employer, or any other information that has been reported to Experian.

8. Your Personal Statement

Any statement that you have added to your report is reflected here. This information remains on your report for a period of two years and is visible to anyone requesting your report. If you have been a victim of identity theft you could use this section to alert creditors, current and prospective.

TransUnion

1. Inquiry Information

Same as "applicant information - provided" reflected above.

2. Demographic Information

This helps to verify the consumer's identity and contains demographic information such as address, date of birth, SSN or aliases used.

3. Alerts

These could include "ID Mismatch", "Fraud Alert", "Fraud Management Program" or "OFAC Name Screen." These are propriety names used by TransUnion to detect potential fraud. If you observe one of these, or any others, on your report contact TransUnion for more information. Do not ignore these or discount them as a reporting error.

4. Model Profile

This displays your credit score. This section is optional and typically incurs a fee as it is not included in the free credit report as required by law.

5. Credit Summary

Provides a "snapshot" of the consumer's credit history. Here is where you would look for any unknown credit accounts.

6. Public Records

Includes public record information maintained in a consumer's file in compliance with the FCRA. Similar to "public records" in the Experian report. Look for any unfamiliar records.

7. Collections

This identifies consumer accounts that have been transferred to collections for debt collection. If you have an account referenced here that you either do not recognize or that you believe to be current, contact TransUnion.

8. Inquiries

As indicated above, inquires into your credit history for the past two years are listed here.

9. Consumer Statement

This contains facts or conditions affecting the consumer's credit history. This information is provided by the consumer and is visible to anyone that requests a copy of the credit history. This would be where you could indicate that you were a victim of identity theft.

10. Credit Report Serviced By

Indicates the bureau that provided the credit history. In the event of a discrepancy, provides contact information to report the discrepancy.

Equifax

1. Application Information - Provided

> Lists name of consumer, date of report request, and confirmation number.

2. Credit Summary

> A summary of account information.

3. Account Information

> Details of credit accounts. This is where you would look for unfamiliar accounts, irregular account balances or past due accounts.

4. Inquiries

> A list of companies that have requested or reviewed your credit history. Typically covers a two year period.

5. Negative Information

> Information that could negatively impact your credit rating is included here, such as bankruptcies, liens, or judgments. Look for any erroneous information.

6. Personal Information

> Personal data, addresses and employment information. Again, look for any discrepancies.

7. Dispute File Information

> Here you'll find instructions on how to dispute information on the report. If discrepancies are detected you must take action. Do not think it is just a reporting error and ignore it. If you do not dispute the information the fraud could continue.

Alerts and Notifications

An alert or notification is designed to bring your attention to something. So why do so many people ignore these? When you receive an alert or a notification pay attention to it and take action. If your credit card has been compromised, request a new one or, in severe cases, close your account. If your bank account has been compromised, close your account. Yes, it is a pain but it will reduce your risk of further exposure.

If you receive a letter that your information has been exposed due to a data security breach, take notice. Find out what the company that experience the data breach is doing to prevent further exposure of your data. Find out what data was exposed. Often times the company will not be able to give you a specific answer. Just verify the type of information - was it a SSN or just your name and address? Many companies will also offer you credit monitoring as a measure of goodwill after a breach. This is good but will not protect you because as credit monitoring only tells you that you are now a victim. Get proactive and check your identity.

Contact the credit bureaus and place a free fraud alert on your account (more on this later) and ask to place information about the breached data onto your credit history report. Remember from in the last section there is a place for you to add personal comments on your credit report.

You could also receive an alert that your credit card company received a change of address request. If you did not initiate this, contact the credit card company and tell them you did not request it.

Being denied credit is another warning flag. If you know your credit is good then get a copy of your credit report. You are entitled to a free one if your credit was denied. Ask the business which bureau they used to obtain your credit history and call the credit bureau. The business should provide you with additional information as it will be needed when you speak with the credit bureau.

If you are notified by mail that your driver's license is suspended yet you have a clean record, better check it out. It is very possible that someone is using your identity and has a counterfeit driver's license with your information on it. Get a copy of your driving record from your state's Department of Motor Vehicles.

If you receive and adverse action letter from a prospective employer it is because of something that was revealed in the background check. The letter will contain information on how to get a copy of the background report or may include a copy of it for you. Review this and contact the consumer reporting agency with any discrepancies.

If you receive a letter regarding a reduction in your credit limit contact the company and ask why. The reason may be listed in the letter. If it was due to something on your credit report, get a copy of your credit report.

Receiving a call from a collection agency for a past due debt is not to be ignored. Ask the caller for as much information as they have on the debt and tell them you may have been a victim of identity theft. There is a good chance they will not believe you so you may just have to hang up to end the call. Then you need to order your credit history reports. Contact the credit bureaus and tell them you suspect you are a victim, explain what happened, and request your report. The collection account should be reflected on at least one of the reports. If you choose to ignore a call such as this, then it will erode your credit score to the point of no repair. You may still be able to repair it but it will take you a lot of time, a lot of patience and perhaps a lot of money in legal fees.

If you receive a letter from the IRS inquiring about unreported income on your tax return and you had reported all of your income you need to contact the IRS. You need to inquire as to the income not reported and the employer information. Request a copy of your consumer report to look for any signs of fraud such as another name associated with your SSN, an address that you do not recognize, or an employer listed that you have never worked for.

These are only a few of the most common types of alerts and notifications received by identity theft victims. Bottom line, if you receive any kind of alert or notification, take action. If you don't, no one else will.

WARNING SIGNS

- Data security breach notification.
- Change of address request notification.
- Denial of credit.
- Notification of suspension of driver's license.
- Adverse action letter.
- Credit limit reduction notification.
- Collection agency call.
- IRS notification of unreported income.

Suspicious Activity

In the animal kingdom, the animals rely on their instinct, their intuition for survival. We humans, however, have decided that we know better and dismiss that little voice telling us that something is wrong. When the hair on the back of our neck is standing on end, why do we so often say to ourselves, "I'm just being paranoid?" Perhaps if we all stopped dismissing these little cues we would be better off.

Case examples

A client was driving down her street when she observed a slow moving vehicle that seemed out of place for the neighborhood. She drove to the end of the road then turned around. As she was driving back to her residence she saw the vehicle parked in front of a house that had been abandoned. She entered her home and contacted the police. The police informed her that there had been a group of individuals driving up and down residential streets stealing mail and breaking into homes. They said they would dispatch an officer to the area. Fortunately she had forgotten to put her mail in her mailbox that day. If she had ignored her intuition she could have put herself at risk, as well as her neighbors.

Here is another example: a man was waiting in line to use an ATM machine located outside of a bank building. The customer in front of him finished her transaction and left. As the man was about to put his debit card into the card reader he became suspicious. He looked at the card reader a bit closer and noticed what appeared to be spray-painting overspray on the reader. Instead of dismissing his suspicions he called the local police. An officer was dispatched and confirmed that a skimmer had been placed on the ATM card reader. Had he ignored his intuition he would have put his account in jeopardy, as the previous customer had done.

If someone has broken into your home don't make the common mistake of only focusing on typically stolen items. You also need to consider that the thief also stole your sensitive documents that were not locked in a secure location. If someone has broken into your home, assume your identity has been compromised and follow the steps outlined in Section five of this book.

If you see suspicious activity, don't just ignore it thinking that someone else will report it, report it yourself. It is better to notify the police and have them say it was nothing than to risk becoming a victim.

WARNING SIGNS

- When the hair on the back of your neck stands up, don't ignore it.
- People slowly driving up and down your street.
- Vehicles that appear out of place.
- Vehicle parked at a residence when you know no one is home.
- Equipment that does not match with the rest of the machine.
- Missing items from your home.
- A broken window.
- An empty trash can when the trash collector has not yet been to your home.
- Your mailbox is empty before the mailman arrives.

Calls About Unknown Purchases

Receiving a call for a purchase you did not make is a warning sign. Especially if it was to congratulate you on purchasing your new Mercedes-Benz and you don't own a vehicle.

What you need to do is get as much information from the company as you can, date of purchase, description, amount paid, store location and anything else the caller can tell you. You should also ask if the purchase was made in person or online. If the purchase was made in person, ask if they have surveillance cameras. If so, you want them to preserve the evidence because you will be contacting law enforcement. You can also ask for the name of the salesperson that sold the item. Thank them for their call and the contact your local police department to file a report.

If the caller will not, or cannot, provide you with any details of the purchase ask him or her for their contact information or contact information for the store. Contact the police and file a report with the information you do have. The sooner you involve law enforcement, the sooner you begin to reduce further exposure.

Make sure to document all calls with, at a minimum, date and time of call, name of person you spoke to and name of the company.

WARNING SIGNS

- Calls for a purchase you did not make.
- Caller cannot provide you with details of purchase.

WORKSHEET

On the next page is a worksheet to track warning signs you have experienced. The worksheet is broken down by statements, credit reports, suspicious activity, and calls about unknown purchases. Enter a description in the appropriate section and then check if you need to follow up or if the item is pending. Once you, or the company holding the account, has completed an investigation, check if the warning sign was due to fraud or error. There are also sections to make notes about the type of warning and account affected, your investigation and the results.

WARNING SIGNS WORKSHEET

Statements	Follow Up	Pending	Notes	Fraud	Error
Checking					
Savings					
Loan					
Other					

Credit Report

	Follow Up	Pending	Notes	Fraud	Error
Experian					
Equifax					
TransUnion					

Alerts & Notifications

Suspicious Activity

Calls About Unknown Purchases

Additional Notes:

NOTES:

NOTES:

I'M A VICTIM, NOW WHAT

Okay, so while reading the last section you detected that you are, or may be, a victim of identity theft. So what do you do now? Here are a few basic steps on the path to restoring your identity. Don't forget to use the checklist at the end of this section.

Credit Bureaus

The three main credit bureaus are Experian, Equifax and TransUnion. These credit bureaus keep track of your credit history. However, they do not all maintain the same information. Not every creditor reports to all three bureaus. This is why it is crucial that you monitor all three of the bureaus to get a better view of your credit history. Credit bureaus will also, when the information has been reported to them, maintain data on your employment history, reported criminal and/or civil records, and various types of public records information. As stated before, it is recommended you obtain a copy of a credit report, credit history, from one bureau every four months rotating the bureaus. This will allow you to receive three free credit reports per year.

After detecting that you are a victim of identity theft, contact one of the credit bureaus and request a free, 90-day "fraud alert" on your credit history. This will reduce the risk of new credit being obtained in your name or negative changes to your credit history. This will not provide 100% protection but is a step in the right direction. Once you have contacted on bureau, that bureau is supposed to notify the remaining two bureaus on your behalf.

You also have the option of extending the fraud alert to seven years if you can prove you are a victim of identity theft. This, as with a security freeze, may delay your ability to obtain credit. Contact each credit bureau to determine the proper documentation required to extend the fraud alert seven years.

When you detect a discrepancy on your credit report, contact the credit bureau that provided the report to dispute the credit report error. Instructions are provided on each of the credit bureau's websites. Look for "disputes" or "credit reporting errors".

Disputes can be reported online, by phone or by mail. I have used the online disputing method and found it to be user-friendly. I also liked the benefit of tracking the status of the dispute online. Believe it or not, my dispute was resolved in less than 24 hours by using the online method. Make sure to have your evidence on hand before disputing the discrepancy. You will need to have specific information, such as dates, times, contact information and the name(s) of the person you spoke with, if any, while disputing an error. This will help expedite your dispute. Once the dispute has been resolved, print out a copy of the dispute status history so you have a 'hard copy' of the document. You may need this information in the future if the same dispute reappears on another credit report.

If you choose to sign up for a credit freeze (also known as a security freeze), contact each bureau (the numbers are listed below). A credit freeze is supposed to prevent any changes or access by creditors to your credit history. I say "supposed to" because again, this is not 100% foolproof. The determination to extend credit is up to the creditor. The creditor can choose to ignore the alert and allow the credit account in your name. There is typically a fee associated with initiating a credit freeze but this can often be waived by submitting a copy of a police report or investigative report. Contact each bureau for additional information. You can also visit www.FinancialPrivacyNow.org for a list of states that allow for a security freeze and applicable fees. The direct link is: http://www.consumersunion.org/campaigns/learn_more/003484indiv.html

Here is the contact information for each credit bureau:

Experian
1-888-EXPERIAN (397-9742)
www.Experian.com

Only available online or by phone.

Equifax
1-800-525-6285
www.Experian.com

Equifax Credit Information Services, Inc
P.O. Box 740241
Atlanta, GA 30374

TransUnion
1-800-682-7289
www.Transunion.com

TransUnion
2 Baldwin Place
P.O. Box 1000
Chester, PA 19022

You can request your credit reports online utilizing www.AnnualCreditReport.com. Remember, this is the only website endorsed by the Federal Trade Commission for obtain credit reports. There are many that claim to offer free reports, such as www.FreeCreditReport.com, owned by Experian, however, they are *not* free and require you to subscribe to credit monitoring.

Another benefit of using www.AnnualCreditReport.com is that you enter your information once and then select the bureau you want to request your credit report. Your report is then viewable online. You can then print or save a copy for your records. I highly recommend you, at the very minimum, print out the credit report. Once printed, you can thoroughly review for any discrepancies. When you are done, file the credit report in a secure location, a three ring binder in a locked file cabinet is recommended. The following year, compare the new report to the current report.

Close Compromised Accounts

Before jumping the gun and closing all of your accounts if you think you've been a victim of identity theft, focus on which accounts have been effected and to what extent. Compromised bank accounts should always be closed. Tell the bank that you want to close your current account and open a similar account with a new bank account number. If a debit/credit/ATM card was compromised, cancel that card and request a new debit/credit/AMT card. If this does not prevent further fraud within 30 days, close your bank account and get a new bank account with a new account number.

If a credit card account was compromised, cancel your current credit card and request a new one with a new credit card number. A credit card account may be a bit more difficult to close especially if you have an outstanding balance. The balance will need to be paid in full before closing the account. If you are unable to pay the balance in full, ask the credit card company to open a similar account for you with a new credit card number and account number. As a last resort, if the credit card company will not assist you then open a new account with a new credit card company and initiate a balance transfer. I recommend you first speak with a representative at the new company and see if they will offer to either waive or reduce the balance transfer fees. Once the balance has been transferred, close your compromised account and ask for confirmation in writing. This can have a negative effect on your credit rating. Anytime you close a long-term established account, you risk a reduction in your credit score. However, a temporary reduction is better then continuing to have a compromised account.

For any other types of accounts, such as loans, utilities, insurance, contact the company directly. Ask for their procedures when handling compromised accounts. Also ask what documentation (to prove the account has been compromised), is required for them to proceed. Most often, a copy of a police report is needed. Even thought the police may not open an investigation, you still need to file a report. You do not need to file a police report each and every incident. Use your judgment. If it was a one time deal and the issue has been resolved, it may not warrant a police report.

For any type of account, if the fraud continues, close the account and get a new account with a new account number. If the fraud affected multiple accounts at the same bank, close all account and move to a different-bank. Remember, you are the consumer and the bank is providing you with a service. If it is not the service you need, find a new service provider.

In Writing Please

Unless communication is documented in writing, it did not happen. Back up any phone conversations with a letter, sent certified return receipt or delivery confirmation. In the letter, include the date, time of call, the name of the representative you spoke with, the problem and the outcome of the conversation. Be a specific as possible. Also, put in the letter what you want the company to do next. Do you want them to reply in writing, or refund your account? If you asked to close an account, state that you want to have written confirmation that the account has been closed. Without written documentation it is your word against theirs.

There are also deadlines when reporting discrepancies (See Section six entitled, Deadlines to Remember). There are a maximum number of days to which a company has to reply to your written request. If the request was made by phone only, the clock does not start ticking. This means the company can take as long as they want in replying to your request. When it is made in writing, the clock starts and the company has to follow the law.

In the resources section of this book you will find a sample copy of a letter of dispute. If you would like a downloadable version, visit my website www.YourPublicIdentity.com. Since you purchased this book, use the code *ypisckg* to register and gain access to downloadable versions of forms, sample letters, monitoring tracking guides and access to my member's only blog, where you can post your questions or read my replies to previously posted questions.

Make sure you keep all written correspondence. This includes email. Put together a file to track your progress and document the outcome. I have found the easiest way to do this is to use a three-ring binder placing the most recent correspondence on top.

Police Report

Most police departments have an Identity Theft Packet listing what to do once you are a victim; samples of letters and affidavits; and instructions on how to complete a police report, also know as an identity theft report. You can also visit the website of the Federal Trade Commission to additional information. The following link provides a wealth of information about filing identity theft reports:

http://www.ftc.gov/bcp/edu/microsites/idtheft/consumers/defend.html#Whatisanidentitytheftreport

If you are told by your local police department that identity theft is not a reportable crime, ask to file a Miscellaneous Incident Report instead. If your local police will not allow you to file an identity theft report, you may have to contact the county police department. If you still are not satisfied, contact your state police department. You can also check with the office of your State Attorney General, www.Naaq.Org, to verify which department is required to take your identity theft report.

Identity Theft Affidavit

An Identity Theft Affidavit is used to dispute accounts that have been fraudulently opened in your name. This is for new accounts. A sample copy of an Identity Theft Affidavit is available at the Federal Trade Commissions website at:

http://www.ftc.gov/bcp/edu/resources/forms/affidavit.pdf

or from TransUnion at

http://www.transunion.com/docs/personal/FTC_ID_affidavit.pdf .

If you are unable to access the form using the above links you can search online for "identity theft affidavit" and many versions of the document will be displayed.

This for may be required to dispute discrepancies in your current accounts as well. Again, you need to contact the company of the account with the discrepancy and ask what documentation is required to dispute the discrepancy.

The IRS also has an Identity Theft Affidavit to use when submitting a discrepancy to the IRS. The form is available for download at http://www.irs.gov/pub/irs-pdf/f14039.pdf

By subscribing to the members only section of my website, www.YourPublicIdentity.com, you will be able to download the above listed documents. Just remember to use the code *ypisckg* when registering.

Federal Trade Commission

The Federal Trade Commission (FTC) has a wealth of information on what to do once you become a victim of identity theft. Their website, while a bit difficult to navigate, provides sample affidavits and letters, many of which are listed in the Reference section of this book. Why reinvent the wheel? Use the sample forms used by them to make your task of restoration easier.

The FTC also collects data on the number of cases identity theft in the United States. I highly recommend that once you have detected that you are a victim of identity theft you visit their website www.ftc.gov to file a complaint. By filing a report, you are helping the FTC gather data on the number and types of cases of identity theft. You are also helping law enforcement catch identity theft criminals. Your data is entered into the FTC's Identity Theft Clearinghouse, a tool used by law enforcement as part of their criminal investigations. You may be contacted by law enforcement if your information becomes part of a criminal investigation.

The FTC also provides information on your rights as an identity theft victim. This information is beneficial when you are dealing with companies that are not cooperating. Unfortunately, some companies hope you do not know your rights and will try to take advantage of you to protect their bottom line. Know your rights and protect YOUR bottom line. Please visit the below link for a summary of your rights as an identity theft victim.

http://www.ftc.gov/bcp/edu/microsites/idtheft/consumers/rights.html

To contact the FTC, visit www.ftc.org or call 1-877-ID-THEFT (438-4338) to report a complaint. You can also write to the Identity Theft Clearinghouse, Federal Trade Commission, 600 Pennsylvania Avenue, NW, Washington, DC 20580. In order to obtain a printed version of your complaint, you must file your complaint online. Copies of the complaint are not provided if you file by phone or by mail.

WORKSHEET

The following page contains a checklist of what to do when you are a victim of identity theft. Please note, this is not a complete list as different types of identity theft require different steps towards resolution. These steps on the checklist are the basic first steps to be used with all types of identity theft.

To use the checklist, enter the date you have completed each step. You will also need to use worksheets provided at the end of this book to document you restoration activities. These include, depending on your situation, "Account Information", "Correspondence and Phone Calls Log" and "Supporting Documentation Log".

If you need additional assistance or if your situation is complicated, I provide consulting services. You can contact me at carrie@YourPublicIdentity.com for more information.

You can also consult the Member's Only section of my website, www.YourPublicIdentity.com, for my answers to questions previously posted by other members and a downloadable format of all of the worksheets in this book.

I'M A VICTIM, NOW WHAT

Date Completed   Place a 90 day fraud alert on your Credit History

Experian	1-888-397-3742
TransUnion	1-800-682-7289
Equifax	1-800-525-6285

Report compromised account(s)

First call then follow up with written letter

Monitor statements for discrepancies

Close Affected Accounts

Request written verification

File a police report

If new account fraud, complete the ID Theft Affidavit

File a complaint with the FTC (choose one option)

1-888-438-4338

www.ftc.gov/idtheft

Use the "Log Sheet" to document your activities

Keep copies of all supporting documentation

Keep copies of all correspondence

NOTES:

DEADLINES TO REMEMBER

There are a few laws you need to know to help limit your maximum liability and to help you monitor your identity for little to no money. These are the EFTA, the FCRA, the FACTA, the FCBA and the FDCPA.

EFTA

The Electronic Funds Transfer Act (EFTA) stipulates the maximum number of days you have to report a discrepancy on your bank statement or report a stolen AMT/debit card to reduce your limit of liability.

Statement discrepancy

If there is an error on your statement, it must be reported to the financial institution, in writing, within 30-60 days from receipt of the statement. It should be noted that some financial institutions have tighter restrictions. For example, one bank states that statement discrepancies must be reported within 15 day of receipt of your statement. If you do not know the time limit for your bank, find out today. If you report it after the deadline, you are liable for the entire amount of the discrepancy.

Lost or stolen ATM/Debit card

- If reported within two days, your maximum liability is $50.
- If reported within sixty days, your maximum liability is $500.
- If reported after sixty days, your maximum liability is unlimited.

There are a few deadlines the financial institution must follow as well.

- 10 days - the number of days they have to investigate your dispute. The ten days begins once they have received written notification from you of the dispute.
- 3 business days - the number of business days the financial institution has to notify you of the completion of your request.
- 1 day - the number of days the financial institution has to replace funds after confirming the dispute.
- 45 days - the number of extension days the financial institution can activate to investigate your dispute.
- Regulation E - doubles the number of days to resolve the dispute to twenty days, and increases the number of days to investigate the dispute to 90 days.

FCRA

The Fair Credit Reporting Act (FCRA) is a complex piece of legislature so I will provide you a basic summary. Below is a list of what the FCRA does for you.

1. Disclose your credit report to you upon request. Consumer reporting agencies (CRA's) must disclose to you the information they have in your file upon request. The CRA's may charge a fee for the report. Some fees are regulated by state or federal guidelines. Instructions on how to obtain the report must be provided when a request has been made. A credit report can be obtained for free once every twelve months from each credit bureau.

2. Limits access to your information. The CRA's cannot release your information to anyone unless they have a permissible purpose. There are various types of permissible purposes allowed but the most common would be obtaining a loan, employment, or applying for credit.

3. Get consent before providing to an employer. An employer must have you sign a release before he can obtain a copy of your credit report.

4. Investigate disputed information. If you detect discrepancies in your report from a CRA, the CRA must promptly investigate the discrepancy. If a resolution is not resolved you may add a comment to your credit history report.

5. Correct or delete incorrect information. If you detect incorrect information on your report the CRA must correct or delete the information, usually within thirty days. This also holds true to information that can no longer be verified.

6. Delete outdated information. Negative information more than seven years old must be removed from your report. Bankruptcies must be removed after ten years.

7. Remove your name from marketing lists. CRA's can provide your name and address to marketing companies whose criteria fit your credit rating. You can opt out of this by calling 1-888-5-OPT-OUT.

8. Disclose your credit score upon request. The CRA must disclose your credit score you upon request. The CRA may charge you a fee for the credit score.

9. You must be told if your file was used against you. If you are denied credit, insurance or employment, or any other adverse action based on the information in your report, you are entitled to receive a free copy of the report from the CRA.

The FCRA also stipulates that once a creditor has received an identity theft report it has four days to block the disputed information from your credit history report. Once blocked, the creditor may not continue to report the information, attempt to collect the debt, or sell to a third party to collect (a debt collector). Reinvestigation will occur within thirty days of receipt of consumer's notification.

FACTA

Fair and Accurate Transaction Act, FACTA, states, among other things, that you are entitled to receive one free credit report from each credit reporting agency (CRA) within a twelve month period.

You are also entitled to receive, for a small fee, a copy of specialty consumer reports. A few examples are listed below.

Consumer credit report

Background check

Tenant check

ChexSystems (banking industry)

MIB (health/life insurance underwriting industry)

State driving record

State criminal record check

Eviction report

Insurance claims report

It should be noted there are many more reports available. In the resources section of this book you will find information on where to obtain these reports.

FACTA states that if you are a victim of identity theft, you are entitled to receive copies of documentation used to commit the crime. These include account applications or transaction records. Any business that provides credit, products or services must provide you with copies of these documents.

FACTA states that change of address requests with replacement card requests must be verified before the address can be changed. The business must take extra steps to validate the change of address request by contacting the cardholder.

For more information on FACTA and protection provided you can view a great summary created by Privacy Rights Clearinghouse at the link http://www.privacyrights.org/fs/fs6a-facta.htm#2b.

FCBA

The Fair Credit Billing Act (FCBA) provides for deadlines and limits of liability when a discrepancy is detected on a statement from a creditor. These would be for "open needed" accounts such as credit cards. When you detect a discrepancy on your credit statement you must send a letter to the creditor within sixty days after the first bill containing the error was mailed to you. It must reach the credit agency before the 60 day window expires. The creditor must acknowledge receipt of your letter within 30 days. The creditor must also resolve your dispute within two billing cycles (but not more than 90 days) after receiving your letter.

Federal law also limits your liability to $50 for unauthorized charges. The law also protects you from billing errors, charges for goods and services you did not accept, goods and services you returned, or charges that list the wrong amount.

FDCPA

The Fair Debt Collection Practices Act (FDCPA) was created to protect consumers from abusive treatment of debt collectors. The law also has a few deadlines to remember when you are contacted by a debt collector for a debt which is not yours.

Within five days of contact a collection agency must provide you with:
- A written statement of what is owed
- The name of creditor

If the information is not accurate:
- You have thirty days from initial contact to dispute the information. Once disputed, the collection agency is not allowed to contact the debtor.

Debt collectors are allowed to contact you by telephone, mail, and/or fax. They can also contact you at home or at work. They can contact third parties to determine your name, address, telephone number and more. If you have any attorney, they must contact your attorney.

Debt collectors are **NOT** allowed to:
- Contact you before 8:00 am or after 9:00 pm
- Reveal your information to third parties
- Harass you or make false statements

NOTES:

A CLOSER LOOK AT IDENTITY PROTECTION SERVICES

Today there are numerous television advertisements, magazine ads, radio ads, and Internet ads for Internet protection. But just how good are they, and do they really offer the protection they claim? Comparing them is like comparing apples to oranges, as each offers different features and benefits. Identity theft protection companies also do not tell you exactly what you are paying for but give you a summary of their services. For example, the company might offer "monitoring of the Internet for your personal identifying information" but how do these companies do it? That is proprietary information that they do not share with you. Sometime the identity protection companies are paying other companies to do the work for them, or perhaps they have developed software to conduct online searches based on specific parameters. Does the company search the surface web or the deep web? Without know the answers to these questions you cannot truly compare products.

This section tries to break down the sales pitch so you know exactly, or as close as possible, what you are buying. I also give you a simple to use format of "pros" and "cons" of each types of service.

Credit Monitoring

Let me start off by saying that credit monitoring will NOT prevent identity theft. Credit monitoring only tells you that you are now a victim of identity theft, and it cannot monitor for all types of identity theft.

Credit monitoring reviews your credit history report and alerts you of any changes to your report. If a new credit account were opened in your name it would trigger an alert. If your bank requested a copy of your credit history report before deciding to offer you a loan, it would trigger an alert. Same thing if an account was transferred to collections, or an account was closed by a creditor.

However, if someone uses your credit card without your permission, no alert is sent since it does not affect your credit history report. If someone buys a counterfeit driver's license with your information it does not trigger an alert. If someone uses your identity at a doctor's office it does not trigger an alert. Now if that unpaid doctor's bill is transferred to collections, then it would trigger an alert. Unfortunately that could be twelve to fourteen months after the damage has been done. If someone steals your mail and check washes your check it, there is no alert.

As you can see, credit monitoring is very limited and only alerts you to changes to your credit history report. If the fraudulent activity does not cause a change in your credit report, you night never know about it.

You can do your own version of credit monitoring for free. As I've mentioned previously, just stagger your requests for your credit reports, one every four months from a different bureau, and you can check it yourself without any additional charges.

Now I am not saying that credit monitoring is a waste of money. In fact, if you have already been a victim of identity theft (more than fraudulent usage of your credit card) then I highly recommend it. Once your information is out there, it will be sold and resold many times over on the personal identifying information black market. By subscribing to credit monitoring, you will be able to jump into action when you receive an alert. But if you have not yet been a victim then you can still do it the free way and review your credit report every four months.

Credit monitoring typically costs around $9.99 per month per subscriber. When purchasing credit monitoring make sure that all three credit bureaus are being monitored. Many companies will only offer you monitoring of one or two bureaus. Forget these and pay more money for all three bureaus. You also want to know if they offer you a free credit report (one from each bureau) every year or if they charge a fee.

Many credit monitoring services now also offer additional monitoring services for the same price. An example of an additional service would be searching the Internet for your name and date of birth. Others claim to monitor the information on black markets for evidence that your information is being sold. Before buying into the hype ask questions. You have a right to know what you are paying for and what you are entitled to.

You also want to pay careful attention to the fine print regarding the Million Dollar Guarantees. A million dollar guarantee is when a company offers to pay you one million dollars if you become a victim of identity theft while a subscriber to their service. Do they have unrealistic requirements in order for you to be eligible for the guarantee? Does the reimbursement cover your out of pocked expenses to restore your identity or the financial losses of the identity theft itself? If you do not understand anything in the contract, ask questions. If your questions are not being answered, pick another company.

Also, once you are a victim, does the company offer any restoration assistance? If they do, what is included? Do they handle the process for you or do they provide you with a help desk support person to walk you through the steps as you do it on your own? What is the training level of the help desk employees that are going to help you restore your identity? Again, ask questions so you know exactly what is included in your subscription.

Pros of Credit Monitoring

- Alerts you of changes in your credit history.
- Allows you to take swift action to restore your identity if detected promptly.

Cons of Credit Monitoring

- You are paying for what you could do just about for free
- Only monitors for fraud relating to your credit history report.
- Does not detect fraudulent usage of your current credit accounts unless transferred to collections.
- Does not monitor driving record.
- Does not monitor fraud from medical identity theft until the account transferred to collections.
- Million guarantees not always guaranteed.
- Many only monitor and not offer any restoration assistance, or only offer limited restoration services.

Identity Theft Insurance

Identity theft insurance policies provide a limited reimbursement of out of pocket expenses once you have become a victim of identity theft. Variations of this are being seen in newer policies. Basically these policies all offer some sort of financial reimbursement if you are a victim of identity theft. Some cover your original loss while others only cover you restoration expenses. Just like with credit monitoring, you need to carefully read the entire policy so you know what you are buying.

Some homeowner's policies include an identity theft policy or make it an exemption. There are also rider policies that can be added to your current policies, and stand alone policies that you can purchase by themselves. I recommend you first review your current insurance policies to see what, if any, identity theft coverage you may already have.

When purchasing a policy, you must look for the amount of the deductible, if any, and limits to the policy. A deductible is the amount you have to pay out of pocket first before the policy will pay. This is in addition to your premiums (your payment to have the policy). The limits of the policy will tell you the maximum amount the policy will reimburse you for your out of pocket expenses. You also need to inquire about any exclusions to the policy. These are items that, under no circumstance, will be covered or reimbursed, by the policy. Another area to check is if the policy has any pre-existing conditions. If you have already been a victim of identity theft you are at a higher risk of becoming a victim again. Insurance companies know this and may charge you a higher premium, exclude specific items, or make you wait a certain period of time before you can use the benefits of the policy.

One more item to consider: Identity theft insurance policies are not a preventive tool. It is a reactive tool. The policy will do nothing to reduce your risk of becoming a victim. It will help you, although limited in nature, once you have become a victim.

Pros of ID Theft Insurance

- Limited reimbursement for out of pocket expenses.
- Good to have if they offer reimbursement of legal fees.

Cons of ID Theft Insurance

- No protection from identity theft.
- Many policies do not cover the financial loss from the fraud, only the out of pocket restoration expenses.
- May have a deductible.
- May only cover financial identity theft and not the other types of identity theft.

Identity Theft Prevention, Protection & Resolution Services

As I said before, if anyone tries to sell you identity theft "prevention" services, walk, no make that, RUN the other way. Identity theft is impossible to prevent. The best you can do is reduce your risk. With that in mind, let's take a closer look at services that claim to offer prevention, protection and resolution services.

Prevention and protection services try their best, with sources available to them, to help you reduce your risk of identity theft. Unfortunately for us, it is much easier for them to sell a product that "protects" something and "prevents" harm from happening. Who wants to buy something that will only reduce the risk? We want full protection! That is why you will see the buzz words "protection" and "prevention" in every advertisement for identity theft services.

What these companies are really selling is convenience. It will handle the monitoring of your public identity for you, check your credit reports, search your identifying information on the Internet, and run your name through various databases to see if there is a criminal record. The company will even review your driving record history and report to you any new activity. And when a warning sign is detected, if the company also offers resolution services, will either initiate the restoration (also know as resolution) process or will guide you through the restoration process. So while I tend to give these businesses a hard time because of word choice in their advertising, I do believe these companies provide a valuable service. That is, as long as you know exactly what you will get for your money.

Resolution, or restoration, services were created to help you restore your identity after becoming an identity theft victim. They may provide you with form letters to send to your credit card company or bank. They may also guide you through the process of initiating a fraud alert on your credit history report. Some even offer to help you amend your medical record if you are a victim of medical identity theft or provide remuneration of out of pocket expenses while restoring your identity. When choosing a restoration company, have a representative tell you, in writing, exactly what the company will do for you. Will you

143

be asked to sign a limited power of attorney so they can mitigate it for you? Or are will the business assign you a contact to walk you through the process? You don't want to find out that you'll receive a "What to do when you are a victim" packet when you were expecting a company to handle the process on your behalf.

You also want to read the fine print to look for any pre-existing conditions. They may only offer a limited amount of assistance if you have already been a victim in the past. They may also have deadlines as to when you must notify them that you are a victim or your contact is null and void.

Pros of Resolution Companies

- Alerts of potential identity theft.
- Limited reimbursement for out of pocket expenses.
- You may be entitled to discounted legal fees.

Cons of Resolution Companies

- Substantial exemptions - read the fine print.
- May exclude coverage for specific types of identity theft.
- Requires you to sign limited power of attorney.
- Does what you can do for little to no money.
- The loss may not be reported in time (remember the deadlines?)
- May provide only guidelines while you do all of the work.
- Limited strictly to standard financial accounts, not liens, judgments or clearing criminal records, etc.
- Once an ID theft victim, you can be a victim again resulting in a new case and new fees.

Identity Theft Restoration Services

Just as the name implies, and as listed briefly in the previous chapter, identity theft restoration services will attempt to restore your identity. Some of services included are credit monitoring, expense reimbursement and access to legal counsel or other professional services. As with the other businesses, make sure you read the fine print. Ask questions. Do they monitor all three credit bureaus or just one? Do they cover medical and criminal identity theft or only financial. The more questions you ask the more you will understand what you are buying.

There are also a few key terms to remember. It is important that you know the difference between resolutions services and restoration services. Resolution services provide you with basic advice over the telephone. These companies do not do the work for you. Restoration services, however, have experienced, qualified staff members who perform the vast majority of the work required to clear your name. Of all of the types of services available, restoration services are the most beneficial. As stated before, it is not a matter of if but when will you become a victim of identity theft.

One recent addition to this category is a restoration service that also tracks down the criminals. This is a new area since most companies just restore your identity and the criminals continue to steal. As an investigator, I like this type of service. If you don't catch the criminals you will never end the cycle.

Pros of Restoration Service

- Best type of identity theft service.
- Someone else does the work to clear your name.
- Experienced and qualified employees.

Cons of Restoration Service

- May only cover financial identity theft.
- Read the fine print - there may be exclusions.
- Requires limited power of attorney.

NOTES:

NOTES:

WORKSHEETS

As you read in the last section, you don't always get what you pay for and often you are paying for something you can do for yourself for little to no money. This section contains worksheets to help you track your information and document your activity after a discrepancy has been detected.

The best way to use the worksheets is to log in to the Member's Only section of my website and download the forms. Print out the forms, as needed, and place them in a three ring binder. The binder, to protect the sensitive information, should be secured at all times, either kept in a locked file cabinet or safe.

1.   **ID Theft Monitoring Worksheet**
     This worksheet will help you keep track of when you have requested and reviewed your records. Two examples are listed at the top of the sheet.

2.   **Account Information Worksheet**
     Use this worksheet to list all of your accounts and corresponding information. This information will be useful if your wallet or purse is stolen. You can list bank accounts, loan accounts, credit card accounts and more. To protect the sensitive information you must secure this document in either a locked file cabinet or safe.

3.   Correspondence and Phone Contacts Log
As stated earlier in this book, when you have a discrepancy you need to take action. You also need to document your actions, the date, the time and the name of the person assisting you. This log will make documentation easier. I recommend you use a new log for each account. If you have discrepancies with two accounts use two worksheets.

4.   Supporting Documentation Log
When dealing with a discrepancy you will be sending and receiving letters, revised statements and other forms of documentation. This document will help you file and later locate the documents.

5.   How to Avoid Becoming a Victim Worksheet
An additional copy of the worksheet provided at the end of the section "How to Avoid Becoming a Victim".

6.   Get Proactive Worksheet
An additional copy of the worksheet provided at the end of the section "Get Proactive".

7.   Warning Signs Worksheet
An additional copy of the worksheet provided at the end of the section "Warning Signs".

8.   I'm a Victim, Now What Checklist
An additional copy of the checklist provided at the end of the section "I'm a Victim, Now What".

For downloadable versions of these worksheets visit my website, www.YourPublicIdentity.com, and subscribe to the Member's Only section using the code *ypisckg*.

Disclaimer: I cannot be held accountable if you request a report and the fee has changed. I have no control over these and am merely giving you the tools to check your identity.

IDENTITY THEFT MONITORING WORKSHEET

Date	Property Records	Driving Record	State Criminal	County Criminal	SSA Report	ChexSystem	Credit Score	Experian	TransUnion	Equifax
1/5/2008									x	
REMARKS	Everything is correct									
REMARKS										
REMARKS										
REMARKS										
REMARKS										
REMARKS										
REMARKS										
REMARKS										
REMARKS										
REMARKS										

Date	Property Records	Driving Record	State Criminal	County Criminal	SSA Report	ChexSystem	Credit Score	Experian	TransUnion	Equifax
REMARKS										
REMARKS										
REMARKS										
REMARKS										
REMARKS										
REMARKS										
REMARKS										
REMARKS										
REMARKS										
REMARKS										

ACCOUNT INFORMATION WORKSHEET

Keep this in a locked - secure location!!!!!!

Institution Name	
Contact Person	
Address	
Phone Number	
Account Type	
Name on Account	
Account No.	
Open date	
Notes	

Institution Name	
Contact Person	
Address	
Phone Number	
Account Type	
Name on Account	
Account No.	
Open date	
Notes	

Institution Name	
Contact Person	
Address	
Phone Number	
Account Type	
Name on Account	
Account No.	
Open date	
Notes	

Institution Name	
Contact Person	
Address	
Phone Number	
Account Type	
Name on Account	
Account No.	
Open date	
Notes	

CORRESPONDENCE & PHONE CONTACTS LOG

Date Time	Contact Name & Phone No	Mailed Letter	Received Letter	Follow-up	Resolved

CORRESPONDENCE & PHONE CONTACTS LOG

Date Time	Contact Name & Phone No	Mailed Letter	Received Letter	Follow-up	Resolved

SUPPORTING DOCUMENTATION LOG

No.	Date	To / From	Original	Copy	Description

SUPPORTING DOCUMENTATION LOG

No.	Date	To / From	Original	Copy	Description

HOW TO AVOID BECOMING A VICTIM

   *   Not currently doing
  **   Needs improvement
***   Doing consistently

Purse/Wallet

	*	**	***
photocopied items			
only carry essentials			
low credit limit			
no SSN card			
no PIN printed			
never leave unattended			
signed credit cards			

Unlocked Mailbox

	*	**	***
incoming mail			
outgoing mail			

Service Providers/Guests

	*	**	***
sensitive info locked/hidden			
file cabinet key hidden			
file cabinet locked			
request criminal backgrounds			

Home Computers   *   **   ***

	*	**	***
password protected			
encrypted wireless network			
screen saver with password			

Pretexting   *   **   ***

	*	**	***
never give sensitive information			
no donations by phone			
no phone surveys			
prizes are free			
don't hire by solicitation only			
grants are not for individuals			
you can't win without an entry			
ask a lot of questions			
have a secret family code word			
contact family members			

Garbology   *   **   ***

	*	**	***
shred, shred, shred			
confetti shredder			
pour liquid on shredded paper			
no prescription labels			
remove device memory			

Technology

	*	**	***
use anti-virus software			
use firewall			
use spam blockers			
use pop-up blockers			
unsolicited email links			
do not click pop-ups			
family internet rules			
talk to kids about internet			
when in doubt, call			
do not forward chain letters			
look before swipe card			
monitor statements			
password on Bluetooth			
encrypt sensitive files			
encrypt USB devices			
password on cell phone			
be selective with apps			
read TOS agreements			
back up cell phone data			
ask if RFID credit card			
cancel RFID credit cards			

Internet   *   **   ***

	*	**	***
private profile			
hidden date of birth			
no family tree			
social networking apps			
no GPS tracking			
no digital diary			
no vacation announcement			
friend only friends			
find your profile			
when in doubt, call			
keep it simple			
read TOS agreements			
ask questions			
encrypt files			
do not file share everything			
search public records			
search the deep web			

GET PROACTIVE WORKSHEET

*   Not currently doing
**   Needs improvement
***   Doing consistently

Monitor Your ID   *   **   ***   Notes

	*	**	***	Notes
Google Alerts				
PIPL				
Clerk of Courts				
Property Appraiser				
Dept. of Motor Vehicles				
State Law Enforcement				
County Law Enforcement				
AnnualCreditReport.com				

Reconcile Monthly   *   **   ***   Notes

	*	**	***	Notes
Checking				
Savings				
Investments				
Loans				
Credit Card				
Equity Line				

Lock It Up   *   **   ***   Notes

	*	**	***	Notes
Locked file cabinet				
Hidden key				

Mail   *   **   ***   Notes

	*	**	***	Notes
Locked mailbox				
Post office box				

Data Storage Devices   *   **   ***   Notes

Password protect/ Encrypt

	*	**	***	Notes
desktop				
laptop				
netbook				
cell phone				
portable storage devices				

Cyber Safety   *   **   ***   Notes

	*	**	***	Notes
Stop-Think-Click				
Think Outside the Web				
Self Monitoring				

Opt Out   *   **   ***   Notes

	*	**	***	Notes
888-5-OPT-OUT				
DMA				

Technology	*	**	***	Notes
use anti-virus software				
use firewall				
use spam blockers				
use pop-up blockers				
unsolicited email links				
do not click pop-ups				
family internet rules				
talked to kids about internet				
when in doubt, call				
do not forward chain letters				
look before swipe card				
monitor statements				
password on Bluetooth				
encrypt sensitive files				
encrypt USB devices				
password on cell phone				
be selective with apps				
read TOS agreements				
back up cell phone data				
ask if RFID credit card				
cancel RFID credit cards				

Internet	*	**	***	Notes
private profile				
hidden date of birth				
no family tree				
social networking apps				
no GPS tracking				
no digital diary				
no vacation announcement				
friend only friends				
find your profile				
when in doubt, call				
keep it simple				
read TOS agreements				
ask questions				
encrypt files				
do not file share everything				
search public records				
search the deep web				

WARNING SIGNS WORKSHEET

Statements	Follow Up	Pending	Notes	Fraud	Error
Checking					
Savings					
Loan					
Other					

Credit Report

	Follow Up	Pending	Notes	Fraud	Error
Experian					
Equifax					
TransUnion					

Alerts & Notifications

Suspicious Activity

Calls About Unknown Purchases

Additional Notes:

I'M A VICTIM, NOW WHAT CHECKLIST

Date Completed   Place a 90 day fraud alert on your Credit History

Experian	1-888-397-3742
TransUnion	1-800-682-7289
Equifax	1-800-525-6285

Report compromised account(s)

First call then follow up with written letter

Monitor statements for discrepancies

Close Affected Accounts

Request written verification

File a police report

If new account fraud, complete the ID Theft Affidavit

File a complaint with the FTC (choose one option)

1-888-438-4338

www.ftc.gov/idtheft

Use the worksheets and logs to document your activities

Keep copies of all supporting documentation

Keep copies of all correspondence

NOTES:

AFTERWORD

As I hope you have learned from reading this book, identity theft is an epidemic and your privacy is dead. One day, if not already, you will become a victim of identity theft. You have learned how to reduce your risk, as now know that you cannot prevent it. I hope that the information in this book has armed you with tools to protect, detect and defend your identity.

Remember, identity theft affects more than just your credit cards. All six types of identity theft: financial, utilities, government documents and benefits, medical, criminal and benefits, can have a great impact on your life, but medical identity theft can be life threatening. As of the writing of this book, there are no effective sources to aid you in the fight against medical identity theft. The best you can do is to monitor your Explanation of Benefit forms from your insurance carrier and medical bills.

Another tool is to think like a criminal. I have reviewed many, but not all, techniques, technical and non-technical, that criminals use to obtain your personal identifying information. This was in an effort to make you think outside of the box, think beyond credit cards and bank accounts. I hope you use the provided worksheet, *"How to Avoid Becoming a Victim"*, as a guide. This will help you find the weaknesses in your armor.

I have also provided you with a few tools to become proactive in the fight against identity theft. Taking a few extra steps to protect your identity is much easier then trying to restore your identity. By using the worksheet, *"Get Proactive"*, you will be able to know what you are doing well and what needs improvement.

I have provided you with common warning signs to help you detect when you may be a victim of identity theft. As stated many times throughout this book, prevention is mission impossible. The best you can do is to detect discrepancies right away so you can take the necessary steps to prevent further damage and begin restoration. Use the worksheet, *"Warning Signs"* to help you locate discrepancies. Once a discrepancy has been found, take action.

Make sure you contact the credit bureaus, close affected accounts, request documentation in writing, file a police report and one with the FTC. If a new account has been opened in your name you will also need to complete the ID Theft Affidavit. By using the *"I'm a Victim, Now What"* worksheet you can track your action step.

But don't forget the deadlines. To better protect you and help you in your recovery you must follow the laws and their deadlines. You also need to make sure your rights are not being violated and that companies are also following the deadlines of the laws.

You don't have to go it alone. There are companies that provide Identity Theft Protection services. I have reviewed the most common types of services and have provided you with the pros and cons of each so you can make an informed decision. It is your money- make sure you are getting your money's worth.

If you are more the do-it-yourself type of person, I have provided you with worksheets which will help you monitor your identity, keep track of your accounts, and document your activity once a discrepancy has been detected.

Identity theft is a threat that will be around for many years. It is not going away anytime soon. I hope this book has been beneficial to you, and you are now armed with the tools to reduce your risk of identity theft.

NOTES:

NOTES:

NOTES:

ABOUT THE AUTHOR

Carrie Kerskie is the president of Marcone Investigations, Inc. based in Naples, FL. She oversees all services provided to clients including corporate investigations, background and asset investigations and Internet and computer investigations. She also directs and performs surveillance for cases involving infidelity, witness location, kidnapping recovery, workers' compensation, and employee theft.

Carrie is a business professional with more than 20 years experience. Prior to owning Marcone Investigations, she worked for some of the top investment and insurance companies in the country. It was in those positions, that Carrie honed the skills and knowledge she would later use to solve some of Marcone Investigations' toughest cases.

Carrie is very active in the community and is a member of the American Business Women's Association Neapolitan Chapter; Florida Association of Private Investigators (FAPI); INTELLENET and Boy Scouts of America.

She has been a guest speaker at conferences, professional and civic organizational meetings, professional development events and corporate training events. In addition, Carrie has developed Internet safety training videos and presentations for parents, individuals and business owners.

Carrie has been featured on *NBC News*, *Wink News*, *ABC News* and *Fox News*. In addition, numerous articles have been written by her and published about her and Marcone Investigations in *Gulfshore Business*, *Southwest Florida Business Today*, *Gulfshore Life*, *Business Currents*, *PI Magazine*, and *Adverse Witness*.

Carrie has also been passionately developing a solution to detect and prevent medical identity theft and healthcare fraud. In 2010 she and her partner, Trevor Briede, discovered the solution- Medical Fraud Defender, which is scheduled for launch in 2011.

She has been recognized with the Harvey R. Morse Founder's Award given for outstanding service to the Florida Association of Private Investigators and the private investigation industry. In 2009, she was selected as one of Gulfshore Business' Top 40 Under 40.

To contact Mrs. Kerskie, email her at Carrie@YourPublicIdentity.com.

7258296R0

Made in the USA
Charleston, SC
09 February 2011

DATE DUE

Genetic Engineering

Other Books in the Current Controversies Series

Genetic Engineering

Susan Henneberg, Book Editor

GREENHAVEN
PUBLISHING

Published in 2017 by Greenhaven Publishing, LLC
353 3rd Avenue, Suite 255, New York, NY 10010

Copyright © 2017 by Greenhaven Publishing, LLC

First Edition

Articles in Greenhaven Publishing anthologies are often edited for length to meet page
requirements. In addition, original titles of these works are changed to clearly present
the main thesis and to explicitly indicate the author's opinion. Every effort is made to
ensure that Greenhaven Publishing accurately reflects the original intent of the authors.
Every effort has been made to trace the owners of the copyrighted material.

Cover image: lightspring/Shutterstock.com

Library of Congress Cataloging-in-Publication Data

Names: Henneberg, Susan, editor.
Title: Genetic engineering / edited by Susan Henneberg.
Description: New York : Greenhaven Publishing, 2017. |
Series: Current controversies | Includes index.
Identifiers: LCCN ISBN 9781534500389 (pbk.) | ISBN 9781534500174 (library bound)
Subjects: LCSH: Genetic engineering--Juvenile literature. | Human reproductive
technology--Juvenile literature. | Food--Biotechnology--Juvenile literature.
Classification: LCC QH442.H46 2017 | DDC 576.5--dc23

Manufactured in the United States of America

Website: http://greenhavenpublishing.com

Contents

Chapter 1: Should the Genetic Engineering of Babies Be Prohibited?

Sally Deneen

Scientists are coming ever closer to the ability to re-engineer human beings. Proponents of genetic engineering claim that parents can choose advantageous genes for their children. Critics warn that redesigning humans and animals will commodify humans and lead to second-class citizenship for those unable to afford the procedures.

Yes: Genetically Modifying Humans Should Be Prohibited

Satyajit Patra and Araromi Adewale Andrew

Scientists do not know enough about human genetics to predict the consequences of modifying the genetic codes. Physical effects can include increased susceptibility to a variety of health issues. Ethicists are concerned about the combination of human with non-human forms. Though the potential is exciting, much more cross-disciplinary debate needs to be conducted.

A Cecile JW Janssens

A new technology called CRISPR-CAS9 allows scientists to insert, remove, and change the DNA of any organism. While it may be possible to prevent disease in certain embryos, personality and intelligence traits are too complex to be edited. Some scientists are calling for a moratorium on human genome modification.

Chapter 3: Is Genetically Modified Food Good for the World?

Chapter 4: Is the Genetic Engineering of Animals Ethical?

US Food and Drug Administration
Genetically engineered (GE) animals contain additional or altered
genetic material intended to give them new traits or characteristics.
Some produce particular substances such as human insulin for
pharmaceutical use. Other animals can become sources of cells,
tissues, or organs that can be transplanted into humans. GE animals
are regulated by the federal government to assure safety for both
animals and humans.

Yes: Genetic Engineering of Animals Is Ethical

Aaron Saenz
The immense bulk of the Belgian Blue cow is due to selectively
breeding animals with a genetic defect. Traditional selective breeding
is being replaced by genetically engineering animals to produce
breeds with advantageous qualities. This technology could potentially
be used in humans.

Bill Pohlmeier and Alison Van Eenennaam
Scientists can use genetic engineering to fight diseases in animals.
Animal breeders can introduce new genetic sequences into livestock
to increase disease resistance. They can remove specific genes that
cause diseases such as mad cow disease. These approaches can
improve animal well-being and increase the production of safer food.

No: Genetic Engineering of Animals Is Not Ethical

Compassion in World Farming
Genetically modifying animals causes high rates of pre- and post-
natal mortality in cattle and sheep. The animals suffer a large variety
of health problems, such as increased susceptibility to infectious
disease. Many scientists conclude that cloning or genetically
modifying animals is not ethically justified.

Yourgenome.org

Among the arguments against GM animals is the risk of new diseases spreading from the GM animals to non-GM animals and humans. The process of modifying animals puts them at risk for pain, deformity, or early death. Some people believe that animals are not a product that can be altered for economic benefit.

Foreword

C ontroversy" is a word that has an undeniably unpleasant connotation. It carries a definite negative charge. Controversy can spoil family gatherings, spread a chill around classroom and campus discussion, inflame public discourse, open raw civic wounds, and lead to the ouster of public officials. We often feel that controversy is almost akin to bad manners, a rude and shocking eruption of that which must not be spoken or thought of in polite, tightly guarded society. To avoid controversy, to quell controversy, is often seen as a public good, a victory for etiquette, perhaps even a moral or ethical imperative.

Yet the studious, deliberate avoidance of controversy is also a whitewashing, a denial, a death threat to democracy. It is a false sterilizing and sanitizing and superficial ordering of the messy, ragged, chaotic, at times ugly processes by which a healthy democracy identifies and confronts challenges, engages in passionate debate about appropriate approaches and solutions, and arrives at something like a consensus and a broadly accepted and supported way forward. Controversy is the megaphone, the speaker's corner, the public square through which the citizenry finds and uses its voice. Controversy is the life's blood of our democracy and absolutely essential to the vibrant health of our society.

Our present age is certainly no stranger to controversy. We are consumed by fierce debates about technology, privacy, political correctness, poverty, violence, crime and policing, guns, immigration, civil and human rights, terrorism, militarism, environmental protection, and gender and racial equality. Loudly competing voices are raised every day, shouting opposing opinions, putting forth competing agendas, and summoning starkly different visions of a utopian or dystopian future. Often these voices attempt to shout the others down; there is precious little listening and considering among the cacophonous din. Yet listening and considering, too, are essential to the health of a democracy. If controversy is democracy's lusty lifeblood, respectful listening and careful thought are its higher faculties, its brain, its conscience.

Current Controversies does not shy away from or attempt to hush the loudly competing voices. It seeks to provide readers with as wide and representative as possible a range of articulate voices on any given controversy of the day, separates each one out to allow it to be heard clearly and fairly, and encourages careful listening to each of these well-crafted, thoughtfully expressed opinions, supplied by some of today's leading academics, thinkers, analysts, politicians, policy makers, economists, activists, change agents, and advocates. Only after listening to a wide range of opinions on an issue, evaluating the strengths and weaknesses of each argument, assessing how well the facts and available evidence mesh with the stated opinions and conclusions, and thoughtfully and critically examining one's own beliefs and conscience can the reader begin to arrive at his or her own conclusions and articulate his or her own stance on the spotlighted controversy.

This process is facilitated and supported in each Current Controversies volume by an introduction and chapter overviews that provide readers with the essential context they need to begin engaging with the spotlighted controversies, with the debates surrounding them, and with their own perhaps shifting or nascent opinions on them. Chapters are organized around several key questions that are answered with diverse opinions representing all points on the political spectrum. In its content, organization, and methodology, readers are encouraged to determine the authors' point of view and purpose, interrogate and analyze the various arguments and their rhetoric and structure, evaluate the arguments' strengths and weaknesses, test their claims against available facts and evidence, judge the validity of the reasoning, and bring into clearer, sharper focus the reader's own beliefs and conclusions and how they may differ from or align with those in the collection or those of classmates.

Research has shown that reading comprehension skills improve dramatically when students are provided with compelling, intriguing, and relevant "discussable" texts. The subject matter of these collections could not be more compelling, intriguing, or urgently relevant to today's students and the world they are poised to inherit. The anthologized articles also provide the basis for stimulating, lively, and passionate classroom debates. Students who are compelled to anticipate objections to their own argument and identify the flaws in those of an opponent read more carefully, think more critically, and steep themselves in relevant context, facts, and information more thoroughly. In short, using discussable text of the kind provided by every single volume in the Current Controversies series encourages close reading, facilitates reading comprehension, fosters research, strengthens critical thinking, and greatly enlivens and energizes classroom discussion and participation. The entire learning process is deepened, extended, and strengthened.

If we are to foster a knowledgeable, responsible, active, and engaged citizenry, we must provide readers with the intellectual, interpretive, and critical-thinking tools and experience necessary to make sense of the world around them and of the all-important debates and arguments that inform it. We must encourage them not to run away from or attempt to quell controversy but to embrace it in a responsible, conscientious, and thoughtful way, to sharpen and strengthen their own informed opinions by listening to and critically analyzing those of others. This series encourages respectful engagement with and analysis of current controversies and competing opinions and fosters a resulting increase in the strength and rigor of one's own opinions and stances. As such, it helps readers assume their rightful place in the public square and provides them with the skills necessary to uphold their awesome responsibility—guaranteeing the continued and future health of a vital, vibrant, and free democracy.

Introduction

> *"Genetic engineering applications are emerging rapidly, producing fierce debates in the US and the rest of the world."*

On July 1, 2016, Vermont became the first state in the US to require the labeling of genetically modified ingredients in most food products on grocery store shelves. This rule had nationwide impact. The US had no regulations regarding GMO food. However, major food companies did not want to manufacture different foods or different labels for one small state. Companies with products such as Campbell soups, Kellogg's cereals, and Mars candy bars put one of these phrases on all their labels: "partially produced with genetic engineering," "may be produced with genetic engineering," or "produced with genetic engineering." Food sold in bulk have labels on shelves or bins. The Vermont law generated a nationwide debate about the safety of eating genetically modified plants and animals. Scientists, however, are concerned about a bigger issue. How can genetic engineering be applied to humans?

Genetically modifying plants and animals is nothing new. For thousands of years, farmers have been modifying plants and animals through selective breeding. Seedless watermelons, purple roses, and purebred dogs are examples of how humans have enhanced desirable traits in organisms. Modern technology has now allowed scientists to modify genes at the molecular level, using gene splicing, gene manipulation, or recombinant DNA technology. Scientists can use enzymes to remove or add DNA to alter genes. Genes from one organism can be removed and inserted into another organism, using a type of "gene gun." For instance, a gene from a bacterium can be inserted into a tomato plant to make it resistant to insects.

Genetic engineering has been widely used in American agriculture. Farmers claim that genetically modified organisms (GMOs) have produced higher crop yields, reduced farm costs, increased farm profits, and brought improvements in health and the environment. In 2016, according to the US Department of Agriculture, 89 percent of corn, 94 percent of soybeans, and 89 percent of cotton was modified to be herbicide tolerant. Farmers can kill weeds without killing the crop. These crops have found their way into American grocery stores in processed foods such as snack foods, sweetened drinks, and breakfast cereals.

GMO proponents say that new crops will benefit consumers around the world. Farmers will be able to grow papayas that repel viruses, corn that survives drought, soybeans that withstand herbicides, and potatoes that don't bruise. GMO supporters claim that as the world population grows, GMO foods will make enough nutritious food to feed everyone despite limited land, water, and other resources.

Not everyone believes that GMO foods are safe or desirable. GMO opponents claim that genetically modified crops can harm the environment. The anti-GMO Institute for Responsible Technology says that GM crops "reduce bio-diversity, pollute water resources, and are unsustainable." Some farmers worry that GMO crops might cross-breed with the naturally existing populations from which they are derived. Consumers who want non-GMO food might not be able to find it. Some scientists are concerned that GMO food could cause dangerous allergic reactions in susceptible people.

Genetically modified animals are another controversial product of the science of genetic engineering. As in plants, genes can be inserted, deleted, or recombined into animal genomes to create animals with select characteristics. GM mice have been used for decades in medical labs to study obesity, heart disease, diabetes, arthritis, substance abuse, aging, and Parkinson disease. GM pigs soon might be suitable organ donors for humans. Goats have been modified to produce malaria vaccine in their milk. Glow-in-the-dark fish can warn people of pollutants in water.

Fast growing salmon, featherless chickens, less flatulent cows, and super muscular pigs have also been developed.

The next step after genetically modifying, some scientists believe, is the cloning of animals. To clone an animal, scientists remove a cell from the animal they want to copy. They then insert the DNA of the donor animal's cell into another animal's egg cell that has had its own DNA-containing nucleus removed. The egg develops into an embryo in the science lab, and then is implanted into a surrogate mother animal. If the mother gives birth, the newborn has the same genetic makeup of the donor animal. This is the process that was used to produce the first cloned animal, Dolly the sheep, in England in 1996.

When news of Dolly's birth was released, scientists, researchers, and many other people became excited about the possibilities in animal cloning. One Korean biotechnology company offered to clone pets for a high fee, though it warned consumers that the animals produced may have different characteristics than the original because of the influence of environment. Livestock producers looked into methods of reproducing particularly high-performing animals. Some scientists researched ways to clone animals that are near extinction before they are lost forever. Cloning animals is notoriously difficult, however, with an average success rate of less than 5 percent.

After Dolly's birth, there was much discussion of the logical next step in cloning, that of cloning humans. Therapeutic cloning, in which human cells are cloned, has shown promise in creating embryonic stem cells. These cells could be used in stem cell therapy to treat diseases, spinal cord injury, blindness, infertility, and more. Another use for therapeutic cloning is to create organs and tissues to improve or replace damaged human tissue. Reproductive cloning is much more controversial. It involves making an entire cloned human, instead of specific cells or tissues. Though many countries and some US states have banned reproductive cloning, in 2015 there were no federal laws banning it in the US.

Genetic engineering applications are emerging rapidly, producing fierce debates in the US and the rest of the world. The controversies are explored in this volume with chapters titled "Should the Genetic Engineering of Babies Be Prohibited?" "Should We Be Afraid of Human Cloning?" "Is Genetically Modified Food Good for the World?" and "Is the Genetic Engineering of Animals Ethical?" Articles from a variety of viewpoints will allow readers to decide for themselves the answers to these important questions.

Should the Genetic Engineering of Babies Be Prohibited?

Overview: Genetic Engineering of "Designer Babies" May Soon Be Possible

Sally Deneen

Sally Deneen is a Seattle-based freelance journalist and editor.

The Human Genetic Blueprint Has Been Drafted, Offering Both Perils and Opportunities for the Environment. The Big Question: Are We Changing the Nature of Nature?

Princeton University microbiologist Lee M. Silver can see a day a few centuries from now when there are two species of humans—the standard-issue "Naturals," and the "Gene-enriched," an elite class whose parents consciously bought for them designer genes, and whose parents before them did the same, and so on for generations. Want Billy to have superior athletic ability? Plunk down the cash. Want Suzy to be exceptionally smart? Just pull out the Visa card at your local fertility clinic, where the elite likely will go to enhance their babies-to-be. It will start innocently enough: Birth defects that are caused by a single gene, such as cystic fibrosis and Tay-Sachs disease, will be targeted first, and probably with little controversy. Then, as societal fears about messing with Mother Nature subside, Silver and other researchers predict that a genetic solution to preventing diabetes, heart disease and other big killers will be found and offered. So will genetic inoculations against HIV. Eventually, the mind will be targeted for improvement—preventing alcohol addiction and mental illness, and enhancing visual acuity or intelligence to try to produce the next Vincent Van Gogh or Albert Einstein. Even traits from other animals may be added, such as a dog's sense of smell or an eagle's eyesight.

What parents would see as a simple, if pricey, way to improve their kids would result, after many generations of gene selection, in a profound change by the year 2400—humans would be two

"Designer People," by Sally Deneen, The Environmental Magazine. Reprinted by permission.

distinct species, related as humans and chimps are today, and just as unable to interbreed. People now have 46 chromosomes; the gene-enriched would have 48 to accommodate added traits, Silver predicts in his aptly titled book, Remaking Eden.

We may already be on the path to change the very nature of nature. If you think it's a far-off prospect best left to future generations, think again. On June 26, 2000, with much fanfare, scientists with the taxpayer-supported Human Genome Project (working with the private Celera Genomics of Rockville, Maryland) announced that they had completed a working draft of a genetic blueprint for a human being. Many details still need to be filled in before scientists can build a human from scratch.

Sequencing the human genome requires identifying 3.2 billion chemical "letters" located on the 46 coiled strands of DNA found in nearly every human cell. While researchers now know the order in which DNA is arranged on the chromosomes, they haven't identified all those chemical "letters," which contain the instructions for making the proteins that comprise the human body. About half of the genome sequence is in near-finished form or better; a quarter is finished. The 15-year project is to be completed in 2005 at a budgeted cost of $3 billion, though some of that tax money is spent on other genomic research.

While the implications for longevity, health insurance and discrimination of this milestone achievement have grabbed media attention, the ramifications for the environment—good and bad— haven't.

An Accelerating Timetable

How soon will all this happen? Silver believes that by around 2010 parents will be able to genetically ensure their babies won't grow up to be fat or alcoholic, and by 2050 arrange to insert an extra gene into single-cell embryos within 24 hours of conception to make babies resistant to AIDS. It is already possible to insert foreign DNA into mice, pigs and sheep. The obstacles to inserting them in humans are mainly technical ones. At this point in human knowledge, it could lead to mutations. Several techniques are under development to try to avoid that, however.

"For the near and midterm future, we're looking at science fiction. You'd have to be terminally reckless to do that type of human engineering on people [with what we know now]," argues law professor Henry T. Greely, co-director of the Program in Genomics, Ethics and Society at the Stanford University Center for Biomedical Ethics.

To change a baby's eye color or hair color within a fertilized human egg "would be a very expensive and dangerous proposition for such trivial purposes," says Dr. Marvin Frazier, who fields human genome questions as director of the Life Sciences Division of the U.S. Department of Energy's Office of Biological and Environmental Research. "It is also my opinion that this would be wrong," he added, "but that will not stop some people from wanting to try."

As for manipulating intelligence or athletic ability, Frazier says it will take scientists many decades to figure out how to do it. These particular traits don't rely on one gene, but on all genes. They also rely "to a significant degree" on nurture instead of nature. Even when scientists figure it out, "It is likely that to achieve the desired goals would require a lot of experimentation, which translates into many hundred or thousands of mistakes before you get it right." That means, Frazier says, "a lot of malformed babies and miscarriages."

A Pivotal Moment

To University of Washington professor Phil Bereano, among others, now is the time for all of us to talk with friends and colleagues to hash out the ethical and societal implications of this Brave New World. Do we really want to commodify people? Could it be a Pandora's box? Unfortunately, the box may already be open: Many nations have banned genetic engineering on humans, but the United States has not.

"If scientists don't play God, who will?" said supporter James Watson, former head of the Human Genome Project, speaking before the British Parliamentary and Scientific Committee in June.

"The key question is not whether human [genetic] manipulation will occur, but how and when it will," says a confident Gregory Stock, director of UCLA's Program on Science, Technology and Society in a report entitled, "The Prospects for Human Germline Engineering."

Meanwhile, a long-anticipated September report by the American Association for the Advancement of Science (AAAS) surprised some observers by failing to call for a ban on making inheritable genetic changes in humans—that is, genetic changes that would be carried on by progeny. Indeed, while the report says that such research "cannot presently be carried out safely and responsibly on human beings," it also leaves wiggle room. "Human trials of inheritable genetic changes should not be initiated until reliable techniques for gene correction or replacement are developed that meet agreed-upon standards for safety and efficacy," says report co-author Mark Frankel, director of AAAS' Scientific Freedom, Responsibility and Law Program.

Noting the public outcry after the cloning of Dolly the sheep—which raised the possibility of cloned human beings—the report stresses the importance of public discussion about genetic research before major technical innovations occur. So instead of a ban, the report suggests "rigorous analysis and public dialogue."

But there's no shortage of opposition to human engineering. The San Francisco-based Exploratory Initiative on the New Human Genetic Technologies seeks, among other things, to alert a largely unwitting public to what is going on. "It really is a nightmare vision," says Rich Hayes, who coordinates the campaign from his Public Media Center office. "Once we start genetically re-engineering human beings, where would we stop? We should have the maturity and wisdom to ban the modification of the genes we pass to our children."

Designer Genes

The futuristic notion of choosing a child's genes from a catalog can certainly capture the imagination. Just as parents today enroll their children in the best possible schools and pay for orthodontics, the parents of the future—perhaps in a few decades—would be able to choose from an ever-increasing suite of traits: hair color, eye color, bigger muscles and so on.

Maybe they'd like to add a few inches to a child's height. Or improve a kid's chances at longevity by tweaking inherited DNA. Or ensure a resistance to viruses. Neighborhood clinics could, by appointment, insert a block of genes into a newly fertilized egg. As one cell broke into two, then four, and so on, each cell would contain the new traits. And the child would pass on those traits to all subsequent generations. Who could blame parents for going for this?

But to Stuart Newman, professor of cell biology and anatomy at New York Medical College in Valhalla, New York, the effect on human biology could be analogous to transforming wild areas into artificial areas, or wild food into artificial food.

We "might be changing people into products—genetically engineered products," says Newman, who also is chairman of the Human Genetics Committee for the Council for Responsible Genetics in Cambridge, Massachusetts. "That's something that's opened up by the Humane Genome Project."

"We believe that certain activities in the area of genetics and cloning should be prohibited because they violate basic environmental and ethical principles," Friends of the Earth President Brent Blackwelder and Physicians for Social Responsibility Executive Director Robert Musil said in a 1999 joint statement. "The idea of redesigning human beings and animals to suit the primarily commercial goals of a limited number of individuals is fundamentally at odds with the principle of respect for nature."

Proponents and critics alike envision a future in which those who can't afford gene enrichment will be relegated to second-class citizenship. "As far as I'm concerned, this thrill we have about the future will end up being one big elitist ripple," says Beth Burrows, director of the Edmonds Institute, a suburban Seattle nonprofit institute that works on issues related to environment, technology, ethics and law.

The Green Dimension

And what about the environment? Burrows says several important questions arise about genetic tampering: What are we creating? How will it affect the natural world? What will be the effect on evolution for each species involved? How will it change feeding patterns, or food for other animals? Without understanding interactions, she says, "We may do some extremely stupid things. If people are concerned that there was such a severe backlash against genetically modified foods, I think they haven't seen anything compared to the backlash when we are able to alter the human genome in significant ways—even insignificant ways," says Burrows.

UCLA's Gregory Stock agrees the impact of human genetic modification is profound, but he likes it. "This technology will force us to re-examine even the very notion of what it means to be human," he wrote in a recent report. "For as we become subject to the same process of conscious design that has so dramatically altered the world around us, we will be unable to avoid looking at what distinguishes us from other life, at how our genetics shapes us, at how much we are willing to intervene in life's flow from parent to child."

Ignacio Chapela of University of California at Berkeley is troubled by still other implications the Human Genome Project may bring for the natural world—including plants engineered specifically to produce human proteins, and pigs produced to have antigens that are more human-like in a quest to help humans. To Chapela, a professor in the Department of Environmental Science, Policy and Management, the concept, say, of using chimpanzees as surrogate mothers for human embryos is "abhorrent—degrading for chimpanzees, and for humans, as well. I think what we're talking about is a very deep understanding of what it means to be part of an intricate web of life, and why we have boundaries between species." To Chapela, proponents see the world as a sphere smeared with mix-and-match DNA. "Evolutionarily, it makes sense to have boundaries," he says, "and we're just willy-nilly breaking them down."

A Brave New World

None of these developments will occur in a vacuum; great advancements in robotics are also expected, portending a trend toward the melding of man and machine in a quest for greater human longevity—to age 110, 130 and beyond. UCLA's Stock dubs this new human/machine "Metaman," a "global superorganism." If it seems like mere musings stolen from a science-fiction film, consider this bit of reality: In March, Berkeley researchers announced that they had invented the first "bionic chip"—part living tissue, part machine. Eventually, such chips and circuitry could help in the development of body implants for treating genetic diseases such as diabetes.

"It's a key discovery because it's the first step to building complex circuitry that incorporates the living cell," mechanical engineering professor Boris Rubinsky, who created the device with a graduate student, said afterward. "The first electronic diode made it possible to have the computer. Who knows what the first biological diode will make possible?"

UCLA's Stock isn't concerned about the effects of human genetic engineering on nature. "Even if half the world's species were lost, enormous diversity would still remain," he argues in his 1993 book, *Metaman: The Merging of Humans and Machines into a Global Superorganism.* "We best serve ourselves, as well as future generations, by focusing on the short-term consequences of our actions rather than our vague notions about the needs of the distant future." If medical science develops an easy cure for cancer, [nuclear] wastes may not be viewed as a significant health hazard after all. If robots can be employed to safely concentrate and reprocess the radioactive materials, they might even be valuable."

Not so fast, says another architect of the modern world, Bill Joy, the father of Java software and co-founder of Sun Microsystems. Joy posits with some feeling of guilt that "our most powerful 21st-century technologies" are threatening to make humans an endangered species." In a celebrated article in Wired magazine last year, Joy blamed the possible extinction of humans on a few key causes, including genetic engineering and robotics. Artificial intelligence should match that of humans within 20 or 30 years.

To combat the perceived inevitability of this Brave New World, Marcy Darnovsky, a Sonoma State University instructor who works with the Exploratory Initiative on the New Human Genetic Technologies, calls for three things: First, a global ban on inheritable genetic engineering on humans; second, a global ban on human reproductive cloning; and third, an effective and accountable regulation of other human genetic technologies.

Burrows says we need to be pondering such weighty questions as: Do we really want to merge with machines? "There are tremendous—awful—choices to be made," she says. "It's very risky to have these discussions because they're about common values. The subject is difficult, painful and easily avoided. But we have to stop focusing on the science and think of ourselves as part of an ecosystem."

Chapela is also worried about the lack of civic discourse. But the advocates are talking, particularly among themselves. At a Berkeley conference, one of them, Extropy Institute President Max More, stood before the crowd and read an open letter to Mother Nature:

> Sorry to disturb you, but we humans—your offspring—come to you with some things to say:
>
> You have raised us from simple self-replicating chemicals to trillion-celled mammals;
>
> What you have made us is glorious, yet deeply flawed.
>
> We will no longer tolerate the tyranny of aging and death. Through genetic alterations, cellular manipulations, synthetic organs, and any necessary means, we will endow ourselves with enduring vitality and remove our expiration date."

Other proponents are more sober, and include Nobel laureate scientists. "This is no 'marginal' movement or way of thinking," Chapela says. "The group advocating human re-engineering includes extremely powerful, influential and wealthy people. So don't expect them to roll over easily or soon."

Genetically Modifying Humans Can Have Unforeseen Consequences

Satyajit Patra and Araromi Adewale Andrew

Satyajit Patra and Araromi Adewale Andrew are on the faculty of the American International Medical University in St. Lucia.

INTRODUCTION

Human genetic engineering relies heavily on science and technology. It was developed to help end the spread of diseases. With the advent of genetic engineering, scientists can now change the way genomes are constructed to terminate certain diseases that occur as a result of genetic mutation [1]. Today genetic engineering is used in fighting problems such as cystic fibrosis, diabetes, and several other diseases. Another deadly disease now being treated with genetic engineering is the "bubble boy" disease (Severe Combined Immunodeficiency). This is a clear indication that genetic engineering has the potential to improve the quality of life and allow for longer life span [2].

Clearly, one of the greatest benefits of this field is the prospect of helping cure illness and diseases in unborn children. Having a genetic screening with a fetus can allow for treatment of the unborn. Overtime this can impact the growing spread of diseases in future generations.

However, these benefits are not without peril. Human genetic engineering is a development that people are either very passionate about or opposed to completely. This article gives a brief account on the effect of this principle on the biosphere together with several controversial issues that accompany the acceptance of this technology [3]. The manuscript has been prepared by using information from peer reviewed journals indexed in pubmed in the period of 2000 to 2015.

Effects on the Environment

Although the positive impacts of this field could be enormous, there are many questions raised that needs to be answered. New organisms created by genetic engineering could present an ecological problem. One cannot predict the changes that a genetically engineered species would make on the environment. The release of a new genetically engineered species would also have the possibility of causing an imbalance in the ecology of a region just exotic species would do. An accident or an unknown result could cause several problems. An accident in engineering the genetics of a virus or bacteria for example could result in a stronger type, which could cause a serious epidemic when released. This could be fatal in human genetic engineering creating problems ranging from minor medical problems, to death [4].

Effects on Human

Looking at the fact that genetic engineering employs viral vector that carries functional gene inside the human body; the repercussion are still unknown. There are no clues as to where functional genes are being placed. They may even replace the important genes, instead of mutated genes. Thus, this may lead to another health condition or disease to human. Also, as defective genes are replaced with functional gene, then it is expected that there will be a reduction in genetic diversity and if human beings will have identical genomes, the population as a whole will be susceptible to virus or any form of diseases [5].

Genetic engineering could also create unknown side effects or outcomes. Certain changes in a plant or animal could cause unpredicted allergic reactions in some people which, in its original form, did not occur. Other changes could result into the toxicity of an organism to humans or other organisms.

Antibiotic Resistance

Genetic engineering often uses genes for antibiotic resistance as "selectable markers." Early in the engineering process, these markers help identify cells that have taken up foreign genes. Although they have no further use, the genes continue to be expressed in plant tissues. Most genetically engineered plant foods carry fully functioning antibiotic-resistance genes.

The presence of antibiotic-resistance genes in foods could have lethal effects. Therefore, eating these foods could reduce the effectiveness of antibiotics to fight disease when these antibiotics are taken with meals. More so, the resistance genes could be transferred to human or animal pathogens, making them impervious to antibiotics. If transfer were to occur, it could aggravate the already serious health problem of antibioticresistant disease organisms [6].

Ethical and Social Issues

"Playing God" has become a strong argument against genetic engineering. Several issues have also been raised as regards the acceptance of this technology. These concerns range from ethical issues to lack of knowledge on the effects genetic engineering may have. One major concern is that once an altered gene is placed in an organism, the process cannot be reversed. Public reaction to the use of rDNA in genetic engineering has been mixed. The production of medicines through the use of genetically altered organisms has generally been welcomed. However, critics of rDNA fear that disease-producing organisms used in some rDNA experiments might develop extremely infectious forms that could cause worldwide epidemics [7].

As more human genes are being used in non-human organisms to create new forms of life that are genetically partly human, new ethical questions arise. For instance, what percentage of human genes does an organism have to contain before it is considered human and how many human genes would a green pepper for example have to contain before it can be eaten without qualms. Human genes are now being inserted into tomatoes and peppers to make them grow faster [8]. This suggests that one can now be a vegetarian and a cannibal at the same time. For meateaters, the same question could be posed about eating pork with human genes. What about the mice that have been genetically engineered to produce human sperm [9]. The question is what psychological effect would it pose on the offspring?

Critics have questioned the safety of genetically engineered bovine somatotropin (BST) to increase the milk yield of dairy cows (BST) for both the cows that are injected with it and the humans who drink the resulting milk; owing to the fact that it increases a cow's likelihood of developing mastitis, or infection of the udder, and it also makes cows more susceptible to infertility and lameness [6].

Transgenic plants also present controversial issues. Allergens can be transferred from one food crop to another through genetic engineering. Another concern is that pregnant women eating genetically modified products may endanger their offspring by harming normal fetal development and altering gene expression [10].

In 2002 the National Academy of Sciences released a report calling for a legal ban on human cloning [11]. The report concluded that the high rate of health problems in cloned animals suggests that such an effort in humans would be highly dangerous for the mother and developing embryo and is likely to fail. Beyond safety, the possibility of cloning humans also raises a variety of social issues like the psychological issues that would result for a cloned child who is the identical twin of his or her parent.

Another frightening scenario is the destructive use of genetic engineering. Terrorist groups or armies could develop more powerful biological weaponry. These weapons could be resistant to medicines, or even targeted at people who carry certain genes. Genetically engineered organisms used for biological weapons might also reproduce faster, which would create larger quantities in shorter periods of time, increasing the level of devastation [12].

Conclusion

Despite all of these current concerns, the potential for genetic engineering is tremendous. However, further testing and research will be required to educate society on the pros and cons of genetic engineering. There is no doubt that this technology will continue to present intriguing and difficult challenges for 21st century scientists and ethicists, and education and meaningful, respectful discourse are just the starting point of what is required to tackle such complex ethical issues. With the newfound breakthroughs in cloning, the capabilities of changing human characteristics are unpredictable. We can then anticipate intense cross-disciplinary debate and discussion as new life forms are emanating through science and medicine [13].

References

1. Patra SAA (2015) Effects of Genetic Engineering - The Ethical and Social Implications. Annals of Clinical and Laboratory Research.
2. Fischer A, Hacein-Bey S, Cavazzana-Calvo M (2002) Gene therapy of severe combined immunodeficiencies. Nat Rev Immunol 2: 615-621.
3. D'Halluin K, Ruiter R (2013) Directed genome engineering for genome optimization. Int J DevBiol 57:621-627.
4. Mercer DK, Scott KP, Bruce-Johnson WA, Glover LA, Flint HJ (1999) Fate of free DNA and transformation of the oral bacterium Streptococcus gordonii DL1 by plasmid DNA in human saliva. Appl Environ Microbiol65:6-10.
5. Jr FW (1996) Viral Genetics. In: Medical Microbiology. 4th Edition edn. University of Texas Medical Branch at Galveston.
6. Mepham TB (2000) The role of food ethics in food policy. The Proceedings of the Nutrition Society 59:609-618.
7. Deuschle K, Fehr M, Hilpert M, Lager I, Lalonde S, et al. (2005) Genetically encoded sensors for metabolites. Cytometry A 64:3-9.
8. Youm JW, Jeon JH, Kim H, Kim YH, Ko K, et al. (2008) Transgenic tomatoes expressing human beta-amyloid for use as a vaccine against Alzheimer›s disease. Biotechnollett30: 1839-1845.
9. Naz RK (2009) Development of genetically engineered human sperm immunocontraceptives. J reprodimmunol, 83:145-150.
10. Smith JM (2003) Seeds of Deception: Exposing Industry and Government Lies About the Safety of the Genetically Engineered Foods You›re Eating.
11. Powledge TM (2002) Will they throw the bath water out with the baby?: The US Congress is still debating whether to outlaw cloning humans. EMBO Reports 3:209-211.
12. Sayler GS, Ripp S (2000) Field applications of genetically engineered microorganisms for bioremediation processes. Curropin in biotechnol 11:286-289.
13. Powledge TM (2002) Will they throw the bath water out with the baby? The US Congress is still debating whether to outlaw cloning humans. EMBO Rep 3:209-211.

Human Traits Are Too Complex to Be Genetically Modified

A Cecile JW Janssens

A Cecile JW Janssens is a research professor of epidemiology at Emory University in Atlanta, Georgia.

This week, scientists gathered in Washington, DC for the International Summit on Human Gene Editing to discuss a technology called CRISPR-CAS9, which can insert, remove and change the DNA of basically any organism. It is relatively simple, inexpensive and accurate, and it's already being used in laboratories around the world to make cells and breed laboratory animals with modified DNA for the study of diseases.

CRISPR could also be used to modify DNA in human embryos, but the question is whether this should be allowed. Among the concerns scientists and bioethicists have highlighted are heritable gene modifications and the use of this technology to create "designer babies." CRISPR provides new opportunities for disease treatment and prevention, but with unknown and potentially substantial risks that warrant an ethical discussion. And this discussion should be rooted in an understanding of what can and cannot be meaningfully edited.

I study the genetic prediction of complex diseases and traits. Research in my field has consistently shown that human traits and common diseases are not genetic enough to be predicted using DNA tests. For the same reasons, it will be impossible to successfully program the presence of traits in embryos.

Any concerns that CRISPR could taken a step further to enhance babies by selecting favorable traits such as intelligence and athleticism may be unwarranted.

What can be edited?

The first (and failed) experiment of human embryo editing aimed to repair a single gene mutation for beta-thalassemia, a severe blood disorder. Other diseases mentioned as future targets for gene editing, such as sickle cell disease and Duchenne muscular dystrophy, are caused by single gene mutations.

These diseases are—at least hypothetically—easier to fix because the cause is entirely genetic and simple. For these diseases, research using CRISPR may lead to breakthrough discoveries for therapies and, potentially, for prevention.

But genetic editing of embryos for single-gene disorders also warrants caution. Not only could off-target cuts—unintended edits in the wrong places of the DNA—introduce heritable errors, but mutations may have so-called antagonistic pleiotropic effects.

This means that the expression of the gene increases the risk of one disease while decreasing the risk of another. Take beta-thalassemia or sickle cell disease, for example: carrying two mutated copies leads to severe illness, but carrying one mutated copy reduces the risk of fatal malaria.

There is still much we don't know about our genome.

Why traits cannot be designed in embryos

For a trait to be "programmed" with gene editing, it needs to meet two criteria.

First, the traits must be predominantly determined by DNA, which means that their heritability needs to be close to 100%. The lower the heritability, the more nongenetic factors such as lifestyle, education and stress play a role. The less likely the trait can be genetically programmed.

Parents who wish to *enhance* their offspring may be particularly risk-averse when it comes to the unknown adverse consequences of genome editing. That means that the heritability of favorable traits may need to be very close to 100%.

But a recent review, summarizing 50 years of heritability research, showed that only a few traits and diseases had an estimated heritability higher than 90%. Intelligence and higher-level cognitive function were around 50%, muscle power at 70% and temperament and personality at around 45%.

Second, the "genetic architecture" must be straightforward. Traits must be caused by a single mutation, like beta-thalassemia, or by an interaction between a limited number of mutations. It may technically become possible to edit DNA accurately at multiple places in the near future. But we still won't know what exactly needs to be edited to program a trait when tens or hundreds of gene variants are involved.

Gene editing for favorable traits is not just a matter of tweaking the genes in the right direction. What makes people intelligent, for instance, isn't a combination of the "right genes" and the "right environment," but the "right combination" of genes and environment. Since the future environment of the embryo is unknown at the moment of editing, it will be impossible to know what the right genes need to be.

This is why the traits people might want to enhance can't be programmed in the embryo, not even with the most accurate and reliable version of CRISPR. The technology is not the limitation for enhancing babies—nature is.

Despite the successes in gene discovery of the past 10 years, our knowledge of the combined contribution of all genetic variants is too limited for embryo editing. Even when all genes and their complex interactions are completely understood, our ability to use gene editing for favorable traits will remain limited because human traits are just not genetic enough.

We need to be clear about what cannot be edited

Urged by concerns about the safety and reliability of CRISPR technology and the unknown medical, societal, environmental and ethical consequences of human gene editing, a group of scientists are calling for a voluntary moratorium on "attempts at germline genome modification of clinical application in humans."

The UNESCO International Bioethics Committee has also called for a moratorium citing concern over the creation of "heritable modifications" and "enhancing individuals." Interestingly, their report acknowledges that CRISPR:

> could be a watershed in the history of medicine [...] even though it must be noted that there are only a few diseases for which the abnormality of one single gene is a necessary and sufficient condition.

This little side note, however, marks the boundaries of what can meaningfully be edited in the DNA of an embryo.

Gene editing technology warrants further study and refinement, which should be accompanied by evaluations of potential adverse consequences. But progress should not be hindered by an ethical debate about a potential misuse of the technology that will not be possible.

Polygenic diseases and traits are simultaneously too complex genetically and not genetic enough. This limits the opportunities for disease prediction, and will also prevent the genetic enhancement of babies.

Genetically Editing Human Embryos Can Have Positive Effects

Julian Savulescu

Julian Savulescu holds the Uehiro Chair in Practical Ethics and is director of the Uehiro Centre for Practical Ethics at Oxford, director of the Oxford Centre for Neuroethics, and director of the Program on the Ethics of the New Biosciences.

Scientists from around the world are meeting in Washington this week to debate how best to proceed with research into gene-editing technology.

Gene editing is a new precise form of genetic engineering. It uses enzymes from bacteria to locate genes within DNA and delete or replace them. In early 2015, Chinese scientists used it to modify human embryos as a first step towards preventing the genetic transmission of a blood disease.

Many people, including scientists, are worried about creating genetically modified humans. They're worried about numerous things: genetic mistakes being passed on to the next generation; the creation of designer babies who are more intelligent, more beautiful or more athletic; and the possibility of causing severe growth abnormalities or cancer.

While these are valid concerns, they don't justify a ban on research. Indeed, such research is a moral imperative for five reasons.

"Five Reasons We Should Embrace Gene-editing Research on Human Embryos," Julian Savulescu, The Conversation, December 3, 2015. http://phys.org/news/2015-12-embrace-gene-editing-human-embryos.html. Licensed under CC BY ND 4.0 International.

1. Curing genetic diseases

Gene editing could be used to cure genetic diseases such cystic fibrosis or thalassaemia (the blood disease that the Chinese researchers were working to eliminate). At present, there are no cures for such diseases.

Detractors say selection of healthy embryos or fetuses via genetic testing is preferable. But such genetic tests require abortion or embryo destruction, which is also objectionable to some people.

What's more, genetic selection doesn't benefit patients—it's not a cure. It merely brings a different person, who is free from disease, into existence. Future people would be gratful if their disease is cured, rather than being replaced by a different healthier or non-disabled person.

2. Dealing with complex diseases

Most common human diseases, such as heart disease or schizophrenia, don't just involve one gene that's abnormal (such as in cystic fibrosis). They're the result of many, sometimes hundreds, of genes combining to cause ill health.

Genetic selection technologies can't eliminate genetic predispositions to these diseases. In principle, gene editing could be used to reduce the risk of heart disease or Alzheimer's disease.

3. Delaying or stopping ageing

Each day, thousands of people die from age-related causes. Cardiovascular disease (strongly age-related) is emerging as the biggest cause of death in the developing world. Ageing kills 30 million every year.

That makes it the most under-researched cause of death and suffering relative to its significance. Indeed, age-related diseases, such as heart disease or cancer, are really the symptoms of an underlying disease: ageing.

Gene editing could delay or arrest ageing; this has already been achieved in mice. Gene editing might offer the prospect of humans living twice as long, or perhaps even hundreds of years, without loss of memory, frailty or impotence.

4. Stopping the genetic lottery

The fourth reason for supporting gene-editing research on human embryos is the flip side of the designer baby objection. People worry that such technology could be used to create a master race, like fair-haired, blue-eyed "Aryans."

What this concern neglects is that the biological lottery—i.e. nature—has no mind to fairness. Some are born gifted and talented, others with short painful lives or severe disabilities. While we may worry about the creation of a genetic masterclass, we should also be concerned about those who draw the short genetic straw.

Diet, education, special services and other social interventions are used to correct natural inequality. Ritalin, for example, is prescribed to up to 10% of children with poor self-control to improve their educational prospects and behavioural control.

Gene editing could be used as a part of public health care for egalitarian reasons: to benefit the worst off. People worry that such technologies will be used to benefit only those who can afford it—keep reading for why they shouldn't.

5. Making disease treatments less costly

Gene editing of human embryos could enable greater understanding of disease and new treatments that don't modify human beings.

Gene-edited embryonic stem cell lines that cause or protect against disease could help us understand the origins of disease. Other edited stem cells could help treatment—imagine blood cells that kill and replace leukemic cells.

This knowledge could be used to develop treatments for diseases, including drugs, that can be produced cheaply. And that would reduce, rather than increase, inequality.

The moral imperative

There are valid concerns about applying gene editing to create live born babies. Such reproductive applications could be banned.

But the technology could be used for therapeutic research: to understand disease and develop new treatments. And any constraints we place on it must keep this in mind.

Laws to prevent reproductive gene editing may be justified on the basis of safety concerns but a ban on therapeutic gene editing cannot.

To ban it would be to ignore a great deal of good that can be done for a great many people, including some of the most vulnerable.

"Designer Babies" Can Have a Positive Impact on Society

Paul Waldman

Paul Waldman is a weekly columnist and senior writer for the American Prospect. *He also writes for the Plum Line blog at the* Washington Post *and the* Week *and is the author of* Being Right Is Not Enough: What Progressives Must Learn From Conservative Success.

Everyone says we don't want new genetic engineering techniques to produce "designer babies." But would that be so bad?

Imagine you knew that you carried a gene for a debilitating illness. But doctors could go into your egg (or your spouse's) and remove that gene, enabling you to have a baby who, whatever other problems they might encounter through their lifetime, wouldn't have to worry about the illness. Would you let them? Most people would say probably yes, provided they were sure the technique was safe and wouldn't produce some kind of two-headed mutant centaur baby. That, after all, is what people were worried about when the first baby conceived via in-vitro fertilization was born in 1978—although in that case, they were worried about cyclops babies (seriously). It turned out in the end that IVF is perfectly safe, and now it's a common procedure, the ethics of which is questioned only by radical anti-choice extremists.

Well we may be approaching the time when doctors can fix certain kinds of inherited diseases before an egg is even fertilized. And naturally, people are worried about "designer babies," the phrase that gets repeated whenever the subject of this kind of genetic engineering comes up. This is a story from NPR yesterday:

"In Praise of Designer Babies," Paul Waldman, The American Prospect, October 10, 2013. Reprinted by permission.

The federal government is considering whether to allow scientists to take a controversial step: make changes in some of the genetic material in a woman's egg that would be passed down through generations.

Mark Sauer of the Columbia University Medical Center, a member of one of two teams of U.S. scientists pursuing the research, calls the effort to prevent infants from getting devastating genetic diseases "noble." Sauer says the groups are hoping "to cure disease and to help women delivery healthy normal children."

But the research also raises a variety of concerns, including worries it could open the door to creating "designer babies." The Food and Drug Administration has scheduled an Oct. 22 hearing to consider the issues.

There are legitimate concerns about safety, and just as with any new medical technique, those have to be thoroughly investigated before this kind of thing becomes common. But is a future of designer babies such a bad thing? I suspect it's one of those things we all assume would be terrible, but we seldom ask *why* it would be so bad.

So let's think about it for a moment. Unless you're a Christian Scientist, a religious sect most of us regard as deranged, no one says to the parents of a sick child, "Well, you just lost the luck of the draw there. It would be against nature to treat your child's illness." So why is it obvious that we should treat the illness after the child is born, but not prevent the illness beforehand?

Perhaps you're concerned about the slippery slope argument—we'll start treating awful diseases, but then quickly move to less critical medical needs, and on to purely elective procedures. But wouldn't the same logic apply? The fact that you might be able to convince a doctor to implant horns on your head isn't a very good argument for not letting a doctor use similar plastic surgery techniques to reconstruct a burn victim's nose. So why is it that we would say that the possibility of genetic engineering being used for something less urgent than preventing a life-threatening illness is a reason to not allow it to be used at all?

And it might be a very good thing to take a few steps down the slope. Genetic engineering of this type is in its infancy, but you could easily foresee a time when we could address all kinds of not life-threatening but still bothersome conditions. If we could free people from things on the order of allergies or myopia, that would be an enormous benefit to them.

One argument you're bound to hear is that technology like this will be distributed unequally, with the rich engineering their superbabies and the rest of of left to have run-of-the-mill children. That's certainly possible, but it depends on the cost of the intervention over the long term, and there's no way to tell yet how expensive it might be in 50 years. Right now we manage to distinguish between necessary medical procedures, which insurance will pay for, and elective ones, which are apportioned on the basis of wealth. Which means that rich people can have more symmetrical noses and perkier breasts and creepily unlined faces than ordinary people do, and that doesn't bother us enough to outlaw plastic surgery. You could envision a time when anyone can get their eggs adapted to remove a slate of harmful conditions and diseases, but only the rich can get the platinum service, which will also give your child shiny, manageable hair. We could probably tolerate that.

I do think we overestimate the degree to which genetic engineering could produce mass inequality. We already have lots of inequality based on genetics. Some people's parents are very smart and some people's parents are extraordinary athletes. Is it unfair that LeBron James' parents gave him the genes that made him six foot eight with loads of natural athletic talent? Not particularly. James himself didn't "deserve" his genetic lottery winnings any more than he would have if his parents were both 5 feet tall and had bought him the body he has through a medical intervention. Furthermore, you could make your next kid that tall, but there are a lot of other variables that would determine whether he actually became the world's best basketball player.

What about intelligence? If we could alter the genes in an egg or a sperm to make a child a bit smarter (which we are a long way from figuring out how to do, by the way), exactly what would be wrong with that? If you had a visceral reaction of opposition when you read that, ask yourself: Why? Try to articulate why it's wrong to use genetic engineering to make a child smarter than they might be if we were just flipping the genetic coin. "Because that's the way it's always been" isn't a persuasive answer. So what is it? Have we violated the free will of the child? Only if you think anyone would choose to be less intelligent than they are; and besides, parents violate their children's free will all the time. The child didn't ask to be smarter, but I didn't ask to have size 10 feet or bad vision; those decisions were made for me. The fact that it was a "natural" process that produced them doesn't make them any more a product of my will.

And it's hard to argue that as a society or a species we have too many smart people. What if a hundred years from now the technology had become safe, cheap, and easy, so a pregnant woman could pop a pill that costs a dollar and would boost her baby's IQ by 20 points—would you think it was wrong then? Keep in mind that parents already do a million things intended to help their developing children become healthier and smarter, some of which begin before the baby leaves the womb.

To repeat, there are serious and complex questions about how safe this kind of genetic engineering would be, and there is a real possibility of unforeseen consequences. But my point is that when we say, "We sure don't want designer babies" as though that's something everyone would naturally agree with, it's worth asking whether our instinctive reaction actually has a rational basis. I'm not a hundred percent sure that we want designer babies. But we might.

CHAPTER 2

Current CONTROVERSIES

Should We Be Afraid of Human Cloning?

Overview: Though Reproductive Cloning Has Ethical Issues, Therapeutic Cloning Shows Promise

Chamundeeswari Kuppuswamy, Darryl Macer, Mihaela Serbulea, and Brendan Tobin

Chamundeeswari Kuppuswamy, Darryl Macer, Mihaela Serbulea, and Brendan Tobin are former visiting research fellows at the United Nations University Institute for Advanced Studies.

Understanding Cloning

Cloning in essence means "making an exact copy." Cloning of cells is a commonplace procedure in the life sciences and reproductive cloning of some animals is now possible. Dolly the sheep was the first such mammal to be born, in 1997.[1] Although there has been some opposition to the cloning of mammals, by and large it has been generally accepted by society, however, it has brought the possibility of the cloning of human beings too close for comfort. While the majority of people do not support cloning of human beings, there are a small minority that do largely base their positions on issues of scientific freedom, reproductive rights and what some see as the inevitability that cloning will someday occur.[2]

Opponents have portrayed reproductive cloning as a violation of human dignity,[3] a position supported by the international community, in the Universal Declaration on the Human Genome and Human Rights (hereinafter "the Universal Declaration") which was unanimously adopted by all member states of UNESCO in their General Conference in November 1997, and unanimously endorsed by the General Assembly in 1998.[4] Article 11 of the Declaration states that "practices which are contrary to human dignity, such as reproductive cloning of human beings, shall not be permitted." Although the Universal Declaration is not a legally

Excerpt from "Is Human Reproductive Cloning Inevitable: Future Options for UN Governance," Chamundeeswari Kuppuswamy, Darryl Macer, Mihaela Serbulea, Brendan Tobin, United Nations University Institute of Advanced Studies, 2007.

binding instrument, it does provide ethical guidance that had global unanimity in 1997, and a number of countries have subsequently adopted legislation banning reproductive cloning.

The global community is split much more evenly with regard to debates over the way to govern scientific research using techniques of human cloning, which do not have the aim of reproduction. This split is in part due to ethical concerns but may also be due to a certain level of confusion over what this term means in practice, the scientific reasons for use of cloning techniques for medical research, and the actual relationship of such research to human reproductive cloning.[5]

While reproductive cloning is meant to result in an animal with the "exact" genetic imprint as the person whose cells are cloned, research cloning[6] is meant to produce tissues, which are an exact match to the person whose cells are cloned. There could be other uses for research cloning, as the name suggests.

Definition of Human Cloning

The Human Genome Organization (HUGO) defines "The term 'cloning,' while used in a general sense to refer to the production of genetic copies of individual organisms or cells without sexual reproduction, involves a number of different techniques, including embryo splitting; somatic cell nuclear transfer into an enucleated egg; and development of cell lines, derived from a somatic cell, in cell culture. Types of cloning may also be distinguished according to the organism in question and to the purpose for which the technique is employed. Human cloning, for example may be subdivided according to the purposes for which it is carried out reproductive cloning, basic research and therapeutic cloning."

The UNESCO/IUBS/Eubios Living Bioethics Dictionary[7] includes the following definitions:

> **CLONE:** A collection of cells or organisms that are genetically identical. An identical genetic copy of an organism—animal/ plant/ human being.

CLONING: The process of asexually producing a group of cells (clones), all genetically identical to the original ancestor. In recombinant DNA manipulation procedures to produce multiple copies of a single gene or segment of DNA. The production of a cell or an organism from a somatic cell of an organism with the same nuclear genomic (genetic) characters—without fertilization.

REPRODUCTIVE CLONING: Use of CLONING technology to produce one or more individuals genetically identical (apart from the genes in MITOCHONDRIA and CHLOROPLASTS) to another individual. In the late 1990s reproductive cloning was used to produce clones of the adults of a number of mammalian species, including sheep, mice and pigs. The most famous of these was DOLLY. Many countries rushed to outlaw the possibility of reproductive cloning in humans. Most bioethicists supported such bans though a minority were more ambivalent.

THERAPEUTIC CLONING / RESEARCH CLONING: Medical and scientific applications of cloning technology, which do not result in the production of genetically identical fetuses or babies.

EMBRYONIC STEM CELLS: (Anglo-Saxon stemm tree or trunk & Latin *cella* storeroom). A formative cell whose daughter cells give rise to other cell types; for example, pluripotent embryonic stem cells are capable of generating all cell types compared to the multipotent adult-derived stem cells which generate many but not all cell types. Thus, stem cells may originate from embryonic tissue and from adult tissue and both types are suitable for cloning technology; that is, therapeutic and/or reproductive. Therapeutic cloning is the cloning of embryos containing DNA from an individual's own cell to generate a source of embryonic stem cell-progenitor cells that can differentiate into the different cell types of the body. The aim is to produce healthy replacement tissue that would be readily available and due to immunocompatibility, the recipients would not have to take immunosuppressant drugs for the rest of their lives. The ethical status of embryonic stem cells is a matter of controversy because the label "embryo" is associated with cloning technology when typically embryonic stem cells are used. Strictly speaking, the early preimplantation blastocyst is not yet an embryo and is more properly called a pre-embryo. For this reason ethics commissions in several nations have approved research on the human pre-embryo up to 14 days because the conceptus is not yet differentiated. In this sense, the pre-embryo cells are no different from those in standard tissue cultures. On the other hand, it is true that a human pre-embryo could, in unscrupulous hands, be guided to develop into a human being. The protagonists against cloning maintain that by virtue of the pre-embryo's special status, it's wrong to carry out destructive experiments on them.

Reproductive Cloning

Reproductive cloning has been common place for some plants that we eat,[8] but it has been possible in animals for less than half a century. After the development of the technique of asexual reproduction of clonal frogs in the mid-1960s there was a period of much debate considering the possibility and ethics of cloning humans. However the 1950s and 1960s experiments in nuclear transfer in amphibians that could generate clones in some species could not be applied to mammals in scientific attempts at nuclear transfer from the 1960s until 1997. Robert Edwards, a pioneer of IVF, suggested in 1984 that making identical human twins could be useful in IVF as twin transfers give higher rates of implantation than single transfers. When it is only possible to obtain a single embryo from collecting eggs, it would increase the chances of a pregnancy if that embryo was split. Animal studies suggest this would present no extra harm to the babies born. In 1993 scientists reported experiments on splitting human embryos, and the growth of these "cloned twins." It has probably been technically possible for a decade. Most mammalian embryos can only be split into 2-4 clones, after that the cells lack the ability to start development into a human being.

In 1997 the paper in *Nature* reported the birth of the first cloned mammal from the transfer of an adult nucleus, "Dolly" the sheep.[9] This followed a paper the year before which made "Morag," the first cloned mammal, also a sheep, made by nuclear transfer from embryonic stem (ES) cells lines into an enucleated egg cell. Both sheep have since died and their stuffed bodies are displayed in the National Museum of Scotland, as symbols of scientific progress. On 24 November 2001 in Worcester, Mass, USA, a company reported in Scientific American "The First Human Cloned Embryo". It included cloned early-stage human embryos—and human embryos generated only from eggs, in a process called parthenogenesis (http://www.sciam. com/). In 2002-2003 the Raelian religious cult claimed that human cloned babies had been born, which is widely thought to be a publicity stunt. No scientific proof or baby has been presented.

Research Cloning

Research or therapeutic cloning as it is often referred to seeks to develop therapeutic remedies for degenerative diseases. This research requires the use of stem cells. Both embryonic and adult stem cells are being utilised in this research. Results from the use of adult stem cells have to date proved generally less favourable than those with embryonic stem cells. There is a general consensus that embryonic stem (ES) cells offer significantly more scientific chances of success than limiting research to adult cells. However, as discussed later, ES cells are controversial to use from an ethical point of view, hard to grow, hard to control (can become cancerous), are rejected in the body unless made to order for an individual by cloning or used in an immune protected site like the brain.

The preference of scientists to work with embryonic stem cells is at the root of research cloning activity which involves the development of embryos as a source of stem cells. This in turn has proved to be the catalyst for opposition to research cloning, opposition which is based on what is seen as the unethical an immoral development of embryo whose sole purpose is to provide stem cells.

In research that has subsequently been retracted, Woo Suk Hwang and colleagues of Seoul National University in Korea announced in the journal Science in February 2004[10] that they had successfully cloned healthy human embryos, removed embryonic stem cells and grown them in mice. This was the first claim that a human embryonic stem cell line could be made by research cloning in humans. They followed this up in May 2005 with claims of the successful cloning of stem cells from patients with Lou Gehrig disease, which showed proof of principle for the concept of making stem cells tailor-made to a patient for therapeutic ends.[11]

The 2004 findings were later shown to be fraudulent in one of the highest profile fraud cases of modern science. The media has been blamed as one of the causes for the widespread utopia that led many to argue for the need for embryonic stem cell research.[12] In spite of the continuous criticisms from bioethicists in Korea regarding the use of junior researchers as egg donors, Hwang was made a national hero and international star, fully supported by the government, mass media and people. Thanks to the information of a whistleblower and the tenacious investigation by the producers of MBC TV, his research was disclosed to be a huge fake. It was fortunate that the verification efforts of young scientists and prompt investigation by Seoul National University brought the case to conclusion. The Korean government hurriedly began to make a guideline for research ethics, and research integrity committees are appearing in many universities. The high profile case illustrates how a transparent research endeavour is necessary.[13]

There were, however, other cases reporting similar research results, but all have found it a major scientific challenge to improve success rates. There have also been reported to be some positive results from adult stem cell research with conversion of cells from one human organ into cells of another.[14] Others have restored normal function to rats whose spinal cords have been cut. Clinical trials using bone marrow to rebuild heart muscle have been successful. Regeneration of adult brain has been seen using adult cells in animals. There has also been a report of making liver cells from bone marrow of an adult—without cloning technology being needed.[15] Having said that, there is still a clear scientific consensus despite the Hwang case from the international community that research should be explored in ES lines because of the promising results to date. Support for ES research has been framed around a variety of themes, including freedom of scientific research, the expectation of medical benefits, and rights of patients to their dignity.

Resources

1. See generally Roslin Institute, http://www.ri.bbsrc.ac.uk/public/cloning.html
2. Amongst the arguments put forward in defence of cloning are those which argue that the cloned individual has a distinct personality, as in the case of identical twins. There are those also believe that human cloning is going to happen sooner or later. Others view a ban on cloning as a restriction of procreative liberty. The argument has also been raised that any impediment to cloning is an infringement of the human right to have children and a family. See Riordan, P.J., Cloning Consensus: Creating a Convention to ban human reproductive cloning, 26, Suffolk Transnat'l L.Rev.411 at 412, where he discusses the potential market and commercial application of the technology; Tully, P, Dollywood Is Not Just A Theme Park In Tennessee Anymore: Unwarranted Prohibitory Human Cloning Legislation And Policy Guidelines For A Regulatory Approach To Cloning, 31 J. Marshall L. Rev. 1385; Kunich Westport, J.C., The Naked Clone: How Cloning Bans Threaten Our Personal Rights, Praeger Publishers, 2003; Katz, K.D., The Clonal Child: Procreative Liberty and Asexual Reproduction, 8 Alb. L.J. Sci & Tech. 1, 40-51 (1997) Also see www.clonaid.com
3. Many scholars have a problem with viewing reproductive cloning as contrary to human dignity. See Caulfield, T., Human cloning laws, human dignity and the poverty of the policy making dialogue, BMC Medical Ethics 2003, 4:3 http://www.biomedcentral.com/1472-6939/4/3. The author argues that on most counts, autonomy, uniqueness, instrumentalisation and replication, reproductive cloning does not violate human dignity. He is of the view that we are in danger of trivializing and degrading the potential normative value of human dignity and

that unless we apply it in a logical and coherent fashion, the notion of human dignity is in danger of being eroded to the point where it stands as nothing more than a symbol of amorphous cultural anxiety. In Beyleveld D, Brownsword R: Human Dignity, Human Rights, and Human Genetics, The Modern Law Review 1998, 61:661-681, Beyleveld and Brownsword feel that "from any perspective that values rational debate about human genetics, it is an abuse of the concept of human dignity to operate it as a veto on any practice that is intuitively disliked." In Wright TG: Second Thoughts: How Human Cloning Can Promote Human Dignity, Valparaiso University Law Review 2000, the author argues against a deterministic conception of a human being and human dignity stating that "Human cloning may well serve to highlight, to emphasise, and to set off with greater clarity, quite apart from anyone's intentions, the mysterious capacities that comprise and express our human dignity." (Quoting from the Article by Caulfield, T.)

4. A/53/152
5. Box 1 lists several definitions of cloning
6. Research and Therapeutic cloning are used alternatively in this paper.
7. Available on website, http://eubios.info/biodict.htm
8. Asparagus is a common vegetable; Orchids are a common flower, reproduced by cloning. Many plants propagate vegetatively in nature, which is the same as cloning
9. Wilmut, I., et al. 1997. Viable offspring derived from fetal and adult mammalian cells. *Nature* 385 (Feb. 27):810
10. Woo Suk Hwang, et al, Evidence of a Pluripotent Human Embryonic Stem Cell Line Derived from a Cloned Blastocyst, Science 303, 1669 - 1674; 2004 (subsequently retracted)
11. Hwang, W. S.., Roh, S. I., Lee, B.C. et al (2005) "Patient-specific embryonic stem cells derived from human SCNT blastocysts," *Science*, 308: 1777-1783.
12. Karori Mbŭgua, Stem Cell Research: Science, Ethics and the Popular Media, Stem Cell Research: Science, Ethics and the Popular Media, *EJAIB* 17 (2007), 6-11.
13. Solbakk, J.H. (2006) "Stem cell research and the ethics of transparency," *Regenerative Medicine* 1 (2006), 831-5.
14. Professor Jonathan Slack at Bath University has managed to convert human adult liver cells into pancreas cells producing insulin, using a simple chemical switch. *Nature Cell Biology,* 2, 879-887, 2000. , 2, 879-887, 2000.
15. May 15, 2002 *Journal of Clinical Investigation.* http://www.jci.org

All Human Cloning Must Be Banned

The US Department of State

The US Department of State directs the official position of the US in all international law.

UNITED STATES STATEMENT - 57 UNGA SIXTH COMMITTEE Agenda Item 165. International Convention Against the Reproductive Cloning of HumanBeings.

Last year, the General Assembly established an Ad Hoc Committee of the Legal Committee to consider the issue of Human Cloning. The Committee met in February and, after hearing the views of a panel of scientists and bioethicists began discussion of the topic. A proposal was presented for a Convention which would prohibit the reproductive cloning of human beings. The United States took the position that a global and comprehensive ban is needed against creation of cloned human embryos for any purpose. President Bush elaborated on this position in addressing the issue in April 2002. The President said, "I believe all human cloning is wrong, and both forms of cloning ought to be banned. Anything other than a total ban on human cloning would be unethical. Research cloning would contradict the most fundamental principle of medical ethics, that no human life should be exploited or extinguished for the benefit of another."

In view of the preliminary discussions of the Ad Hoc Committee, which indicated a divergence of views on the proposal, the proponents of the convention to ban human reproductive cloning have slightly modified their proposal. They now suggest "a step-by-step" approach to these complex bioethical issues. First, there would be a ban on reproductive cloning of human beings. This could then lead, at a later stage, to "measures concerning the

"Views of the United States on Cloning," USUN, U.S. Department of State, September 23, 2002.

regulation of other types of cloning by interested States, including through the elaboration of a separate international instrument." They argue that such an approach would make it quite clear that a Convention against the reproductive cloning of human beings should not be seen as implicitly authorizing all types of cloning.

The United States does not agree. A ban that prohibited only "reproductive" cloning but did not address "therapeutic" or "experimental" cloning would implicitly authorize the creation and destruction of human embryos for experimentation. Furthermore, a ban on reproductive cloning would be impossible to enforce in an environment that permitted therapeutic cloning in laboratories. Once cloned embryos were available, it would be virtually impossible to control what was done with them, including the implantation of a cloned human embryo and bringing that embryo to term as a new cloned human. Indeed, even in the face of a ban on reproductive cloning, the scientist could export the cloned embryos to a jurisdiction where no such ban existed.

The proponents of a convention to ban human reproductive cloning have expressed concern that an attempt to achieve a ban on all types of cloning would undermine efforts to conclude a convention before a cloned human is produced. This view assumes that a convention could be negotiated and brought into force in a very short period. Recent conventions produced by the UN General Assembly have taken several years to enter into force. To ban "reproductive" cloning effectively, all human cloning must be banned. Under a partial ban that permitted the creation of cloned embryos for research, human embryos would be widely cloned in laboratories and assisted-reproduction facilities. Once cloned embryos were available, it would be virtually impossible to control what was done with them. Stockpiles of embryonic clones could be produced, bought and sold without anyone knowing it. Implantation of cloned embryos would take place out of sight, and even elaborate and intrusive regulations and policing would have great difficulty detecting or preventing the initiation of a clonal pregnancy. Once an illicit clonal pregnancy is begun, it would be virtually impossible to detect it. A ban only on "reproductive" cloning would therefore be a false ban, creating the illusion that such cloning had been prohibited. Furthermore, a completely effective ban would require universal acceptance to ensure that there were no safe havens for cloning activities.

It would be shortsighted to ignore the reality of this situation in the search for a solution through a step-by-step process, a process that would attempt to use two instruments, two regimes to deal with different aspects of a single problem, cloning, and which would take years to conclude. We must thwart this threat to human dignity through a total ban.

The United States, therefore, continues to support a ban on all human cloning and urges immediate action by the UN to put such a ban in place. We cannot agree to start down the road of a step-by-step process that would prohibit the production of cloned human beings but not prohibit the production of cloned human embryos for immediate destruction, an equal affront to human life and dignity.

In February the U.S. delegation presented a detailed description of the U.S. position. We would be pleased to provide copies of that paper to any delegation requesting it.

USUN September 23, 2002

The Views of the United States on the Science and Ethical Implications of Human Cloning

A. *The United States' Position*

The United States supports a global and comprehensive ban on human cloning through somatic cell nuclear transfer, regardless of the purpose for which the human clone is produced. The United States believes that so-called "therapeutic" or "experimental" cloning, which involves the creation and destruction of human embryos, must be part of this global and comprehensive ban. Thus, the Untied States does not support a ban that is limited merely to "reproductive" cloning.

Any ban on human cloning should explicitly state that it does not prohibit the use of nuclear transfer or other cloning techniques to produce DNA molecules, organs, plants, tissues, cells other than human embryos, or animals other than humans.

In addition, we believe that nations should actively pursue the potential medical and scientific benefits of adult stem-cell research. Such research does not require the exploitation and destruction of nascent human life, nor does it open the door to the dehumanizing possibilities that will come with the cloning of human beings.

B. Scientific Background

Cloning refers to any process that results in the creation of an identical or nearly identical genetic copy of a DNA molecule, cell, or individual plant, animal, or human. Cloning occurs in nature. For example, identical twins are the product of a natural cloning event. There have also been recent scientific developments in cloning, such as the 1997 live birth of a sheep created using an experimental cloning method called "somatic cell nuclear transfer."

Somatic cell nuclear transfer is a cloning technique used by scientists to produce a nearly genetically identical copy of an existing animal. The product of somatic cell nuclear transfer is an embryo. In simple terms, this embryo is created by replacing the nucleus of a female egg cell with genetic material from a "somatic" cell (which is a cell from the body other than a sperm or egg cell). There is no involvement of sperm. The resulting embryo is a clone that is nearly genetically identical to the donor of the somatic cell. (Since the donor egg also contains non-nuclear DNA in subcellular structures called mitochondria, the clone's cells contain a very small amount of mitochondrial DNA from the donor egg cell. Thus, the clone is not exactly genetically identical to the somatic cell donor.)

Scientists conduct two types of experiments using somatic cell nuclear transfer. The first type of experiment, sometimes described as "reproductive" cloning, involves the creation of an embryo through cloning, and its subsequent implantation into the uterus with the objective of creating a living animal. Animal reproductive cloning experiments have very high failure rates (around 95%) and often result in stillbirths, spontaneous abortions, or offspring with severe congenital abnormalities.

The other kind of experiment, sometimes described as "research," "experimental," or "therapeutic" cloning, involves the creation of a cloned embryo, which is then used to derive stem cells or (after the embryo is grown to a fetal stage) tissues for transplantation. For example, after the embryo grows to the blastocyst stage (5-9 days), the embryo is destroyed in order to derive embryonic stem cells that may hold the potential for the development of cell replacement therapies. (Stem cells are discussed more fully in the attachment.) Hypothetically, therapies based on stem cells derived from cloned human embryos would not be subject to immune rejection if transplanted into the human donor of the somatic cell used for cloning. Other kinds of research on cloned embryos have also been attempted. Recently, researchers have reported that they have grown cloned animal embryos in an animal host uterus beyond the blastocyst stage and successfully extracted differentiated tissue for replacement therapy.

Whatever its purpose, cloning through human somatic cell nuclear transfer necessarily involves the creation of a living human embryo. For this reason, the technique raises profound ethical and moral questions and is highly controversial.

There are other cloning techniques that do not raise these moral and ethical concerns. For example, scientists routinely employ cellular or molecular cloning in their work to make genetically identical cells for research. Although these other cloning techniques could be used to develop therapies to treat disease, scientists do not use the term "therapeutic" to describe these techniques. Rather, as discussed above, the term "therapeutic" cloning is used by scientists to describe cloning by somatic cell nuclear transfer for therapeutic, as opposed to reproductive, purposes. This latter type of cloning is also described as "experimental" cloning, or "cloning for research purposes."

C. Ethical Implications of a Partial Ban on Human Cloning

Human cloning—for any purpose—is an enormously troubling development in biotechnology. It is unethical in itself and dangerous as a precedent.

The possible creation of a human being through cloning raises many ethical concerns. It constitutes unethical experimentation on a child-to-be, subjecting him or her to enormous risks of bodily and developmental abnormalities. It threatens human individuality, deliberately saddling the clone with the genetic makeup of a person who has already lived. It risks making women's bodies a commodity, with women being paid to undergo risky drug treatment so they will produce the many eggs that are needed for cloning. It is also a giant step toward a society in which life is created for convenience, human beings are grown for spare body parts, and children are engineered to fit eugenic specification.

We cannot allow human life to be devalued in this way. A proposal has been made to ban only so-called "reproductive" cloning, by prohibiting the transfer of a cloned embryo into a woman to begin a pregnancy in the hopes of creating a human baby. This approach is unsound.

First, a ban that prohibited only "reproductive" cloning, but left "therapeutic" or "experimental" cloning unaddressed, would essentially authorize the creation and destruction of human embryos explicitly and solely for research and experimentation. It would turn nascent human life into a natural resource to be mined and exploited, eroding the sense of the worth and dignity of the individual. This prospect is repugnant to many people, including those who do not believe that the embryo is a "person."

Second, to ban "reproductive" cloning effectively, *all* human cloning must be banned. Under a partial ban that permitted the creation of cloned embryos for research, human embryos would be widely cloned in laboratories and assisted-reproduction facilities. Once cloned embryos are available, it would be virtually impossible to control what was done with them. Stockpiles of embryonic clones could be produced, bought and sold without anyone knowing it.

Implantation of cloned embryos, an easy procedure, would take place out of sight, and even elaborate and intrusive regulations and policing could not detect or prevent the initiation of a clonal pregnancy. Once begun, an illicit clonal pregnancy would be virtually impossible to detect. And if detected, governments would be unlikely to compel the pregnancy to be aborted or severely penalize the pregnant woman for allowing the implantation or for failure to abort the pregnancy. A ban only on "reproductive" cloning would therefore be a false ban, creating the illusion that such cloning had been prohibited.

Third, a ban that permits embryonic clones to be created and forbids them to be implanted in utero legally*requires* the destruction of nascent human life and criminalizes efforts to preserve and protect it once created, a morally abhorrent prospect.

Fourth, there may be other routes to solving the transplant rejection problems, and there is to date no animal research to support the claim that cloned embryonic stem cells are therapeutically efficacious. A legal ban on "therapeutic" cloning would allow time for the investigation of promising and less problematic research alternatives such as "adult" stem-cell research. It would also allow time for policy makers and the public to develop more informed judgments about cloning, and for the establishment of regulatory structures to oversee applications of cloning technology that society deems acceptable.

There are other cloning techniques that do not raise these moral and ethical concerns. For example, scientists routinely employ cellular or molecular cloning in their work to make genetically identical cells for research. These other cloning techniques—that do not entail the creation and destruction of human embryos—are currently being used to develop therapies to treat disease. Any ban on human cloning should explicitly state that it does not prohibit the use of nuclear transfer or other cloning techniques to produce molecules, organs, plants, tissues, cells other than human embryos, or animals other than humans.

We believe that States should actively pursue the potential medical and scientific benefits of adult stem-cell research. Such research does not require the exploitation and destruction of nascent human life, nor does it open the door to the dehumanizing possibilities that will come with the cloning of human beings.

The United States does not support a ban limited to "reproductive" cloning. We believe that so-called "therapeutic" or "experimental" cloning, which involves the creation and destruction of human embryos, must be included.

Thus, the United States supports a global and comprehensive ban on human cloning through somatic cell nuclear transfer, regardless of the purpose for which the human clone is produced. We look forward to working with other delegations to achieve that objective.

Attachment: Stem Cell Overview

Cloned human embryos produced through somatic cell nuclear transfer are potentially a source of human embryonic stem cells. They could also be used for other experimental purposes. This attachment provides some information about embryonic and adult stem cells.

Stem cells are cells that occur in animals at all stages of development, front the embryo to the adult. They have different properties and abilities, depending on the age of the organism and the location of the stem cells within the organism.

Embryonic stem cells are derived from a 5-9 day-old embryo and are able to generate nearly all the cell types of the body. To date, human embryonic stem cell research has been conducted using stem cells derived from embryos that were created in the course of in vitro fertilization and were no longer needed for that purpose.

Adult stem cells occur in small numbers throughout the bodies of adult mammals. Under normal conditions, they generate the cell types of the tissue in which they reside. Under certain experimental conditions in the laboratory, or even after transplant into a living animal, adult stem cells may be able to differentiate into the specialized cells of several different tissues.

All stem cells are unspecialized (undifferentiated)—they do not have any specific structures that allow them to perform specific functions such as carry oxygen or fire an electrical signal. Unlike specialized cells such as muscle cells, blood cells, or nerve cells, which divide slowly or not at all, stem cells are also capable of dividing and renewing themselves for long periods (self-renewing). Importantly, stem cells retain the unique ability to give rise to specialized cells (differentiation), such as muscle, skin, or neurons.

Scientists believe that human stem cells—embryonic and adult, differentiated to specific cell types—offer the possibility of a renewable source of replacement cells and tissues to treat a myriad of diseases.

Human Cloning Crosses Numerous Ethical Boundaries

Sophia M. Kolehmainen, JD

Sophia Kolehmainen, JD, MSEL, is the Human Genetics Program Director for the Council for Responsible Genetics ("CRG"). CRG is a national nonprofit organization made up of scientists, lawyers, academics, and concerned citizens dedicated to broadening the debate about the use of the new genetic technologies. The organization is based in Cambridge, Massachusetts, and focuses on two main program areas: commercial biotechnology and the environment and human genetics.

Introduction

Until recently, discussions about human cloning were conducted within the realm of science fiction and fantasy. However, with the successful cloning of the sheep "Dolly" in 1997, it became evident that sooner or later, scientists might be able to clone human beings, too. This possibility has incited both support and opposition. Newspapers and magazines have described cloning as an exciting step forward that allows genetic engineers to reduce the uncertainties of reproduction, but they have also published commentaries by scientists, religious figures, and others who see human cloning as an attack on human dignity. This Essay focuses on whether we as a society should accept human cloning by somatic cell nuclear transfer to create offspring.

Cloning: The Science of Controversy

Somatic cell nuclear transfer is the cloning technique that was used by the Scottish scientists to produce Dolly. It involves the removal of DNA from an egg-cell and fusion of that enucleated

"Human Cloning: Brave New Mistake," by Sophia M. Kolehmainen, Council for Responsible Genetics. Reprinted by permission.

egg with a differentiated cell from an already existing organism, like a skin cell, or in the case of Dolly, a mammary cell from a sheep which had been dead for six years. The Scottish scientists found that fusing the two cells with an electric shock triggered a "reprogramming" which caused the combined egg-mammary cell to divide and mature like an early embryo.

Cloning technology developed as a way to improve the production of genetically engineered animals. There are huge financial profits to be made by developing genetically engineered animals that secrete chemicals and proteins of value to humans, such as cows or goats that produce human blood clotting agents in their milk. Without cloning, scientists must genetically manipulate each individual animal, which results in very low success rates. However, with cloning comes the possibility that scientists need only perfect one animal to clone an entire herd from that success. The goal is not to copy everything about the animal, only the property that has been engineered into it. The desire of some genetic engineers to gain control over the innermost workings of animals fueled the further development of cloning technology. It is out of this context that some people are now attempting to justify human cloning.

The transfer of cloning techniques to humans, however, creates a host of unique technical, ethical and social issues that aren't currently raised in the cloning of animals. Whereas the point of cloning animals is to create more economically efficient bio-factories of identical animals with value to humans, cloning humans is being suggested as a procreative technique to copy existing people.

In 1998 reporters covered Richard Seed's declaration that he intended to raise the funds to produce two to three copies of himself through cloning. This announcement illustrates the false view held by many that cloning will result in exact copies of existing, or dead, individuals. This is just not true. The cloning process would never produce an exact copy of the cloned person. Though an individual manufactured by cloning would posses the same genetic sequence as the person whose nucleus was used other factors also substantially affect the development of an individual. An individual's development may be affected by structural and metabolic influences of the enucleated egg and the differentiated cell, as well as influences during gestation. In addition, non-genetic factors such as nutrition, home environment, education, economic situation, and culture add significantly to the development of personhood. Just as with animals, cloning humans will never produce exact copies.

Other false views persist in the language of cloning, namely equating cloning with reproduction, and equating cloning with the birth of identical twins. A cloned individual would be one made by scientists, using a pre-existing genetic configuration, without the joining of gametes from two people. The cloning process is not sexual reproduction, but is more akin to asexual replication of organisms that simply split in two. The production of a clone is vastly different from the process by which twins are born. So-called identical twins, though genetically identical to one another, have two genetic parents, and are still biologically unprecedented in that their genetic configuration has never existed before.

Brave New Mistake

It would be a mistake to develop and use cloning as a technique to replicate human beings. It is questionable what benefits would be gained from the successful creation of a cloned human being, if any, and whether they would justify the radical impact cloning would have on our society. Cloning is not just another reproductive technology that should be made available to those who choose to use it, but is an unnecessary and dangerous departure from evolutionary processes and social practices that have developed over millions of years. As with many other developments in biotechnology, some scientists and commentators are asking us to accept cloning of humans just because it is technically possible, but there are few good reasons to develop the technology, and many reasons not to develop it.

1. Safety Concerns

The most frequently stated argument against cloning is based on safety concerns. After the news of Dolly, President Clinton convened the National Bioethics Advisory Commission (NBAC) to review the legal and ethical issues of the potential cloning of a human. The NBAC heard testimony and read opinions on the multitude of complex issues surrounding human cloning, but in the end, the NBAC based its recommendation for a three to five year moratorium on human cloning in the United States on safety concerns.

At this point in the process of experimenting with cloning, safety is an important concern. The production of Dolly required at least 276 failed attempts. No one knows why these attempts failed and why one succeeded. Cloning presents different obstacles in every species, as embryo implantation, development, and gestation differ among different species. Human cloning therefore could not become a reality without extensive human experimentation. Though 276 "failed" lambs may be acceptable losses, the ethical implications of failed or partially successful human experiments are unacceptable.

Inhibitions concerning human experimentation would seem to be an impassable ethical and practical barrier to human cloning, but there may come a time when scientists feel they have enough knowledge from animal experiments to proceed with human trials. Even if questions of safety could be eliminated, which is highly unlikely, or if public opinion and scientific hubris were to reach the point where the risks associated with human experimentation seemed less egregious, human cloning should still be prohibited for several reasons.

2. Commodification

Cloning would encourage the commodification of humans. Though industrialized societies commodify human labor and human lives, the biological commodification involved in human cloning would be of a vastly different order. Cloning would turn procreation into a manufacturing process, where human characteristics become added options and children, objects of deliberate design. This process of commodification needs to be actively opposed. It produces no benefits and it undermines the very basis of our established notions of human individuality and dignity.

3. Human Diversity

Cloning would also disrespect human diversity in ethnicity and ability. Though it is not possible to produce exact copies of animals or people, inherent in cloning is the desire to do so. The process of cloning would necessarily increase conformity, and eradicate genetic variety. A society that supported cloning as an acceptable procreative technique, would imply that variety is not important. Especially in a multicultural nation like the United States, where diversity and difference are of the essence, any procedure that reduced our acceptance of differences would be dangerous. It is clear from the tensions that exist in our society that we should be embracing processes that increase our appreciation for the diversity of individuals, not working to remove differences.

4. Permanent Changes to the Gene Pool

The process of cloning would inevitably invite the use of other genetic technologies, specifically genetic manipulation of cloned embryos, and this could result in permanent, heritable changes to the human gene pool. Some scientists pretend that they can predict which genes humans would be better off without. However, there is no way to acquire the requisite genetic knowledge to make such a prediction without experimental genetic manipulation, which would have implications for subsequent generations. Such experiments must not be done, since both the errors and supposed successes of genetic manipulation would be with humanity forever. Although the potential applications of human genetic engineering may appeal to some, the experimental nature of the technique, and the permanence of the results, would make it a highly dangerous innovation.

5. *Threat of Eugenics*

Cloning would allow for genetic manipulation that sets the stage for increased efforts at eugenics. Eugenics is the attempt to improve human beings, not by improving their economic, social, and educational opportunities, but by altering the genes with which they are born. Cloning would allow scientists to begin with a known human prototype (the person to be cloned) and then "improve" it by modifying specific traits. People who wanted to be cloned could have themselves cloned only to be taller, blonder, smarter. The threat of eugenics is inherent in technologies that allow individuals to try to modify inherited characteristics so as to give preference to specific ones. It would be impossible to embark on human cloning without opening the door to eugenics. After all, cloning in animals by "improving" their inherited characteristics is a deliberate form of animal eugenics.

6. *Natural Procreation and Evolution*

Ordinary procreation, whether it results in twins or singletons, is an open-ended process that depends on the random coming together of an egg and sperm cell. Each new individual has a unique configuration of genes which leads to an amazing range of human variability. Cloning forecloses the opportunity for genetic surprise and growth among cloned humans, limiting such future people to genetic configurations that have been expressed before.

Cloning Is Not a Reproductive Answer

The discussion above provides a strong basis to support a prohibition on human cloning. Cloning developed in the context of animal commodification and the technique's intent and purposes are not applicable in humans. Even setting aside the fact that cloning cannot produce exact copies, and that it cannot go forward without much prior human experiment, the above arguments weigh heavily against ever allowing the cloning of humans.

In addition, there are no clear, defensible arguments in favor of offering cloning as an option for producing offspring. Cloning is endorsed by some as a procreative technique that provides a cure to infertility or an option for people who have genes they do not want to pass on and the chance to have genetically related offspring for gay and lesbian couples or people without partners. Such arguments are not convincing.

Their flaws stem from the fallacy of their premise and their neglect of the availability of other, less questionable, options. First, if cloning were in fact a "cure" for infertility, then infertility would no longer exist. Newborns, elderly people, women who have had complete hysterectomies, and people born without ovaries or testes would all be able to bear offspring. In reality, cloning does nothing to alleviate the underlying environmental or social causes of infertility. Labeling cloning as a cure for infertility implies the acceptance of entirely new definitions of fertility and infertility, and is therefore misleading. Technically, cloning is replication of that which already exists. It is not a "cure" for anything.

Current reproductive technologies offer couples who have genes they don't want to pass on, or gays, lesbians, and people without partners an array of alternatives to cloning. People can choose genetic testing to avoid transmitting certain genes to their offspring. Lesbians, gays, and unpartnered people can acquire sperm, eggs, embryos and gestational ("surrogate") mothers. Adoption is another option.

Problems associated with rising rates of infertility will not be solved through the development of high-tech, invasive and expensive interventions. Even now, rather than answering the needs of people unable to reproduce, many of the new technologies used in assisted reproduction actually create needs and make it increasingly difficult for people to accept other, less complex and invasive solutions. The psychological problems associated with infertility are created by societal as well as by personal pressures, and should be understood and dealt with at that level.

Some proponents of human cloning who recognize the weakness of their arguments, continue to support the development of human cloning under the banner of freedom—freedom of reproductive choice and freedom of scientific inquiry. They argue that people should have the choice to produce offspring in this way, and scientists should have the option to explore human cloning without outside interference. With these arguments, proponents of human cloning are able to side-step the lack of clear benefits of this technology by raising a banner to "freedom" and "choice."

The ill-defined boundaries of a person's right to procreative autonomy makes some people cautious about prohibiting cloning. The NBAC report noted that a prohibition on cloning would be in tension with the fundamental right to procreate. The right to privacy and some level of autonomy in decision-making about procreation can be traced through a series of Supreme Court decisions. Generally speaking, this line of cases supports the notion that the decision whether to bear or not to bear a child is one which is of the most personal and private nature and should therefore be made without governmental interference. Some cloning proponents have extended this right to mean that the government has an obligation to support the development of all techniques that may help citizens reproduce.

This is an improper expansion of the right to be free from governmental interference in reproductive decision-making. A prohibition on cloning does not interfere with that right because the government does not have the obligation to ensure that each citizen who wants a child has a child. The right covers only the right of individuals, who can reproduce, to reproduce (or not) without government interference. Providing and safe-guarding the option to clone, in the face of the numerous negative implications of the technology, is not an acceptable justification to support the technique.

Another argument used to counter a prohibition on cloning is that it would stifle scientific inquiry. But, science is not an unbiased, objective field of study, and not all scientific possibilities need be accepted by society. Scientific research is conducted by people with personal and professional interests in the outcome and continuation of their work. It is often motivated by a quest for profits and power. A prohibition on human cloning may indeed make it more difficult for scientists to study some inherited genetic diseases, though that is far from clear. However, allowing cloning in order to meet this hypothetical need would radically alter our current concepts of humanity and of procreation. Not all scientific inquiry has equal priority and the question should be who gets to set the priorities; scientists, their funders, or the public. Like other publicly supported activities, science must serve the public interest and the public should have the power to influence decisions about which paths are worth exploring.

Cloning

The cloning debate, like the debates surrounding the introduction of many of the new genetic technologies, often reflects the proposition that if science can do something, it should be done. Scientists introduce new technologies with inflated promises of potentially solving the world's problems—genetically engineered crops to end world hunger, or mapping the human genome so as to end disease. Researchers and their investors promote these technologies without proof of actual benefit or lack of harm. In reality, many of these "miracle" inventions could cause harm, and to date few of the promised benefits have been realized.

Human cloning represents another one of these false "miracles." It would cure no disease while it would markedly alter our relationships to each other and the natural world. Human cloning cannot proceed without crossing numerous ethical boundaries. With no identifiable benefit to the technique, existing social and legal arguments against it should not be set aside, and human cloning should therefore be permanently banned.

Human Cloning Should Be Embraced

Russell Blackford

Russell Blackford is conjoint lecturer in philosophy at the University of Newcastle, Australia. Blackford is a fellow with the Institute for Ethics and Emerging Technologies, a laureate of the International Academy of Humanism, and editor-in-chief of the Journal of Evolution and Technology.

Dolly, the world's most famous and controversial sheep, was born twenty years ago—on July 5, 1996 to be precise. She was the first mammal to enter the world following a process of reproductive cloning, making the event a spectacular scientific breakthrough.

To create Dolly, researchers at the Roslin Institute in Scotland employed a technique known as somatic cell nuclear transfer (SCNT). With SCNT, DNA from the nucleus of an ordinary cell—obtained from anywhere in an animal's body—is transferred into an enucleated oocyte (egg cell), typically from a different animal.

In Dolly's case, her DNA came from one sheep's mammary cell; it was implanted into an egg from another sheep; and the resulting tiny biological entity was implanted into the uterus of yet a third sheep, where it grew until birth.

The result of SCNT is a creature with almost the same genetic potential as the one providing the nuclear DNA. SCNT is thus a powerful, and often effective, form of animal cloning.

Dolly is born! Announcement and reaction

Subsequently, in February 1997, Ian (now Sir Ian) Wilmut and his research team at the Roslin Institute announced Dolly's birth in the prestigious science journal *Nature*. This provoked political and ethical debates that have never truly stopped.

Public discussion of cloning gradually receded in prominence as new issues arose to dominate the airwaves and the headlines, notably the threat of jihadist terrorism following the attacks on September 11, 2001. But issues relating to cloning technology remain crucial to debates over biomedical research and its regulation.

The announcement—with a description of the method used to bring Dolly into existence—triggered a feverish worldwide response because of the possible implications for human cloning. It was immediately obvious that SCNT could, in principle, be used to create human babies. Across the world, many countries banned human cloning—often with significant punishments, such as lengthy jail terms, even for attempting such a thing.

The case against cloning

The actual arguments against human cloning are extremely varied, and I cannot elaborate them all here. (I go into more of them, and in far more depth, in my 2014 book, *Humanity Enhanced: Genetic Choice and the Challenge for Liberal Democracies*).

One common claim is that bringing children into the world in this way is somehow a violation of the natural order, or of human dignity; or perhaps it would be an act of "playing God." Unfortunately, it can be very difficult to pin down precisely what any of these claims really mean in the context of bioethical debate. I am, for example, sceptical about the existence of anything that can correctly be called "human dignity."

Some critics fear that children created via SCNT would be subjected to unfair expectations of duplicating the talents and achievements of whoever provided their nuclear DNA. Sometimes the critics speak in terms of the autonomy of the child being violated, diminished or denied, although it can be very difficult to spell out exactly what this amounts to. In *Humanity Enhanced,* I challenge the idea that children conceived through SCNT would have their autonomy violated—or would somehow lack or lose autonomy—in any sense inapplicable to "ordinary" children.

Some critics worry about a larger social effect, or even an effect on our species, if cloning restricted the diversity of children being born (perhaps because parents and doctors might look for donors with a narrow range of characteristics, such as possessing high intelligence and meeting certain standards of physical beauty).

Yet other arguments acknowledge that reproductive cloning in itself might not have a great social or species-wide impact; however, it's claimed, cloning could place human societies on a slippery slope toward accepting even more radical technological interventions such as genetic engineering of human traits. On one version of the approach, this would, in turn, set us upon a path to unequivocally horrible social outcomes. Thus cloning supposedly confronts us with a slippery slope to another slippery slope ... which seems like a tenuous style of argument.

Though some of these fears may have an element of truth, they are all exaggerated. In my view, which I've defended in *Humanity Enhanced* and other publications, human cloning would not be a seriously worrying action if we could carry it out safely.

To some extent, however, all of this is moot. Over the past twenty years, we have enjoyed success in cloning many mammalian species, but no one has cloned a human being. Indeed, we have been frustrated in efforts to clone other primates such as apes and monkeys.

In the upshot, human reproductive cloning is not yet feasible, and indeed there's no current prospect that it could be carried out effectively and safely in the foreseeable future. Even if we did conceive a human embryo through SCNT, and we then managed to bring it to term, the odds are very high that the result would be a seriously deformed child.

That's a good pragmatic reason not to make attempts until we know a lot more, and even then we'd need to have developed the technology to a point where we are about as likely as with ordinary births to end up with a healthy baby.

I don't rule out that someone might accomplish this technological feat one day, but, once again, there is no sign of it happening. Nor is it what SCNT research is really about from the point of view of reputable medical researchers. The real action is with what is known as "therapeutic cloning." Allow me to explain.

Reproductive and therapeutic cloning

So far I've focused on "reproductive cloning," and more specifically on human reproductive cloning: the postulated use of SCNT (or any other technique that might have a similar result) to bring about the birth of a human child.

By contrast, the expression "therapeutic cloning" refers to the creation of human embryos by SCNT for some other purpose, such as for biomedical research or for harvesting cells or tissues to be used in therapies.

Although some ethical issues are raised with therapeutic cloning—including a concern that the associated research destroys human embryos—the idea has been obtaining legal acceptance in some countries, usually subject to tight government regulation. If we start to see impressive results from therapeutic cloning, with new therapies emerging from the research, I expect that it will eventually obtain the same wide acceptance that IVF—in vitrofertilization—now enjoys in Western countries. (It's not that long ago that IVF was also widely regarded as abhorrent.)

More generally, people come to embrace new technologies, even those that initially seemed shocking and "unnatural," once concrete benefits become clear.

Twenty years later

Two decades later, I'm not sure that the ethical arguments advanced for and against human cloning are greatly different from those we saw back 1997. However, the early debate was very one-sided. The initial response to the dramatic *Nature* article by Wilmut et al. was largely one of fear, mingled with disgust, with too little rational reflection. Since then, the fear-mongering has partly died down, but not before a great deal of draconian legislation was enacted across the world. Little chance was given for calmer voices—or any dissenting voices—to be heard before governments took action.

As it seems to me, calmer voices eventually won the academic debate. There is a strong sense, within the field of secular bioethics, that the early arguments against human reproductive and therapeutic cloning were flawed. However, dissenters lost the politicaldebate almost before it began. Politicians, journalists, many academics, and the general public in our Western liberal democracies greeted the very idea of human cloning with a cascade of hostility.

The expressions of fear, disgust, and moral outrage appeared immediately; in response, highly illiberal laws were enacted without due consideration of the issues.

But more reasonable people are slowly winning back the central political ground, gradually making the public case that technologies based on SCNT may bring many benefits. That, perhaps, will be the story of the next twenty years.

Human Cloning Offers Medical Benefits

Jayashree Pakhare

Jayashree Pakhare is a science writer and teacher.

The process of creation of genetically identical person from either a living or dead person is known as human cloning. It includes the production of clone tissues, also donated from the individual to be cloned. This term refers to artificial human cloning only. The birth of twins is called natural human cloning. Even though the birth of twins is the result of natural human cloning they are separate people with separate experience. The presence of identical DNA makes no difference in their being different personalities. The scientific community all over the world is still investigating the question how similar the original and its clone would be and this may depend up on how much of personality traits are determined by genes. Scientists have managed to clone animals like Dolly, the sheep. They have obviously tried the same method on humans, and have reached considerable success. However, many countries and governments have banned human cloning fearing the ill-effects of human clones. The human race is not yet prepared to come face-to-face with clones moving about with normal people. There is a huge debate on the pros and cons of human cloning. This Buzzle article on human cloning will cover the advantages of cloning humans.

Techniques of Human Cloning and Claim of Success

The most common technique used in human cloning is "somatic cell nuclear transfer." Under this technique, the nucleus of an egg cell taken from a donor is removed. Then, the original cell gets fused with another cell of same genetic material to be cloned.

"Human Cloning Benefits," Buzzle, Reprinted by permission.

Another technique used, is parthenogenesis. This technique involves inducement of unfertilized egg to divide and grow as if it were fertilized. As recently as on May 2005, a team of scientists led by Mr Hwang Woo-Suk attached to Seoul National University, claimed to have created 11 lines of human stem cells using a different technique. [This claim was later determined to be fraudulent.]

Benefits of Human Cloning

There are some ways by which human cloning can benefit the humankind. Here is a list of advantages.

Cloning People

One of the main reasons why human cloning turns out to be a scary affair, is that it would allow people to clone themselves. Just imagine, you could get a twin by cloning yourself. Parents who lose their children to death may get tempted to clone their dead child. Some may think of cloning Einstein or Usain Bolt and give rise to a league of superhumans or super-sportsmen. Those against humanity may give rise to clones of the famous villains in of our history. Although the idea of a clone sounds pretty attractive, no one knows how the clone will behave and will he/she develop similar personalities like its master clone.

Rejuvenation

It has been found that the production of clone tissue should be helpful in making aging people look young. According to Dr. Richard Seed, one of the leading proponents of human cloning technology, one day it should be possible to reverse the aging process.

Heart Attack Treatment

Today, heart attack is the number one killer in the developed as well as developing countries. Scientists believe that by cloning healthy heart cells and injecting them in to the damaged heart area, they can treat heart attacks.

Human stem cells

It has been experimented that nascent cells can be grown to produce human organs or tissues. This can be used for repairing or replacing the damaged organs. A combination of human stem cells production and human cloning technology can be used to produce tissues for suffering people, which are otherwise rejected by their immune system.

Infertility treatment

The success rate of current infertility treatments is very low. Further, the couple has to go through tormenting procedures with a small chance of getting a child. The advent of cloning technology will make it possible for infertile couples to have [children more] than ever before.

Use in Surgeries

Presently silicon gels and other cosmetics are being used in surgery. These materials not only suit the patients but also cause immune disease. In human cloning, doctors, instead of using materials foreign to the body are able to grow cells, bones, tissues that match that of person taking treatment. Victims of terrible accidents with deformed faces can hope to have their features repaired with safe technology. The case of breast implants for cosmetic reasons is also similar. With the silicone implants, people developed illness of their immune system.

Defective genes

It is estimated that an average person has 8 defective genes inside him. People with defective genes will develop illness in spite of their keeping good health otherwise. With cloning, it is possible to have genes without any defects.

Other benefits

By switching cells on and off through cloning, it has been found that cancer can be cured. The phenomenon of cells differentiating into specific kinds of tissue was baffling the scientists. Cloning may hold the key in making them understand differentiation and cancer. Down's syndrome, liver failure, kidney failure, leukemia, spinal cord injury, genetic diseases are some of the ailments which can also be cured by cloning.

The success stories of human cloning and creating tissue cells have come from different parts of the world. People have also been treated with the technology and have started to realize some benefits of cloning. The response and feedback the Human Cloning Foundation has been getting is a testament of the popularity this form of science is getting all over the world. But, many countries have not accepted this. The human cloning has not been given legal status in many countries. However, the stem cell research has been accepted by some governments. Till the scientific community comes up with a legally acceptable human clone, God, the creator of all human beings, born and to be born, can continue to enjoy, the status of a "creative maverick"!

CHAPTER 3

Is Genetically Modified Food Good for the World?

Overview: The Safety of Genetically Modified Food Continues to Be Assessed and Debated

World Health Organization

The World Health Organization directs and coordinates international health within the United Nations' system.

Frequently asked questions on genetically modified foods

These questions and answers have been prepared by WHO in response to questions and concerns from WHO Member State Governments with regard to the nature and safety of genetically modified food.

1. What are genetically modified (GM) organisms and GM foods?

Genetically modified organisms (GMOs) can be defined as organisms (i.e. plants, animals or microorganisms) in which the genetic material (DNA) has been altered in a way that does not occur naturally by mating and/or natural recombination. The technology is often called "modern biotechnology" or "gene technology," sometimes also "recombinant DNA technology" or "genetic engineering." It allows selected individual genes to be transferred from one organism into another, also between nonrelated species. Foods produced from or using GM organisms are often referred to as GM foods.

2. Why are GM foods produced?

GM foods are developed—and marketed—because there is some perceived advantage either to the producer or consumer of these foods. This is meant to translate into a product with a lower price, greater benefit (in terms of durability or nutritional value) or both.

Initially GM seed developers wanted their products to be accepted by producers and have concentrated on innovations that bring direct benefit to farmers (and the food industry generally).

One of the objectives for developing plants based on GM organisms is to improve crop protection. The GM crops currently on the market are mainly aimed at an increased level of crop protection through the introduction of resistance against plant diseases caused by insects or viruses or through increased tolerance towards herbicides.

Resistance against insects is achieved by incorporating into the food plant the gene for toxin production from the bacterium Bacillus thuringiensis (Bt). This toxin is currently used as a conventional insecticide in agriculture and is safe for human consumption. GM crops that inherently produce this toxin have been shown to require lower quantities of insecticides in specific situations, e.g. where pest pressure is high. Virus resistance is achieved through the introduction of a gene from certain viruses which cause disease in plants. Virus resistance makes plants less susceptible to diseases caused by such viruses, resulting in higher crop yields.

Herbicide tolerance is achieved through the introduction of a gene from a bacterium conveying resistance to some herbicides. In situations where weed pressure is high, the use of such crops has resulted in a reduction in the quantity of the herbicides used.

3. Is the safety of GM foods assessed differently from conventional foods?

Generally consumers consider that conventional foods (that have an established record of safe consumption over the history) are safe. Whenever novel varieties of organisms for food use are developed using the traditional breeding methods that had existed before the introduction of gene technology, some of the characteristics of organisms may be altered, either in a positive or a negative way. National food authorities may be called upon to examine the safety of such conventional foods obtained from novel varieties of organisms, but this is not always the case.

In contrast, most national authorities consider that specific assessments are necessary for GM foods. Specific systems have been set up for the rigorous evaluation of GM organisms and GM foods relative to both human health and the environment. Similar evaluations are generally not performed for conventional foods. Hence there currently exists a significant difference in the evaluation process prior to marketing for these two groups of food.

The WHO Department of Food Safety and Zoonoses aims at assisting national authorities in the identification of foods that should be subject to risk assessment and to recommend appropriate approaches to safety assessment. Should national authorities decide to conduct safety assessment of GM organisms, WHO recommends the use of Codex Alimentarius guidelines (See the answer to Question 11 below).

4. How is a safety assessment of GM food conducted?

The safety assessment of GM foods generally focuses on: (a) direct health effects (toxicity); (b) potential to provoke allergic reaction (allergenicity); (c) specific components thought to have nutritional or toxic properties; (d) the stability of the inserted gene; (e) nutritional effects associated with genetic modification; and (f) any unintended effects which could result from the gene insertion.

5. What are the main issues of concern for human health?

While theoretical discussions have covered a broad range of aspects, the three main issues debated are the potentials to provoke allergic reaction (allergenicity), gene transfer and outcrossing.

Allergenicity

As a matter of principle, the transfer of genes from commonly allergenic organisms to non-allergic organisms is discouraged unless it can be demonstrated that the protein product of the transferred gene is not allergenic. While foods developed using traditional breeding methods are not generally tested for allergenicity, protocols for the testing of GM foods have been evaluated by the Food and Agriculture Organization of the United Nations (FAO) and WHO. No allergic effects have been found relative to GM foods currently on the market.

Gene transfer

Gene transfer from GM foods to cells of the body or to bacteria in the gastrointestinal tract would cause concern if the transferred genetic material adversely affects human health. This would be particularly relevant if antibiotic resistance genes, used as markers when creating GMOs, were to be transferred. Although the probability of transfer is low, the use of gene transfer technology that does not involve antibiotic resistance genes is encouraged.

Outcrossing

The migration of genes from GM plants into conventional crops or related species in the wild (referred to as "outcrossing"), as well as the mixing of crops derived from conventional seeds with GM crops, may have an indirect effect on food safety and food security. Cases have been reported where GM crops approved for animal feed or industrial use were detected at low levels in the products intended for human consumption. Several countries have adopted strategies to reduce mixing, including a clear separation of the fields within which GM crops and conventional crops are grown.

6. How is a risk assessment for the environment performed?

Environmental risk assessments cover both the GMO concerned and the potential receiving environment. The assessment process includes evaluation of the characteristics of the GMO and its effect and stability in the environment, combined with ecological characteristics of the environment in which the introduction will take place. The assessment also includes unintended effects which could result from the insertion of the new gene.

7. What are the issues of concern for the environment?

Issues of concern include: the capability of the GMO to escape and potentially introduce the engineered genes into wild populations; the persistence of the gene after the GMO has been harvested; the susceptibility of non-target organisms (e.g. insects which are not pests) to the gene product; the stability of the gene; the reduction in the spectrum of other plants including loss of biodiversity; and increased use of chemicals in agriculture. The environmental safety aspects of GM crops vary considerably according to local conditions.

8. Are GM foods safe?

Different GM organisms include different genes inserted in different ways. This means that individual GM foods and their safety should be assessed on a case-by-case basis and that it is not possible to make general statements on the safety of all GM foods.

GM foods currently available on the international market have passed safety assessments and are not likely to present risks for human health. In addition, no effects on human health have been shown as a result of the consumption of such foods by the general population in the countries where they have been approved. Continuous application of safety assessments based on the Codex Alimentarius principles and, where appropriate, adequate post market monitoring, should form the basis for ensuring the safety of GM foods.

9. How are GM foods regulated nationally?

The way governments have regulated GM foods varies. In some countries GM foods are not yet regulated. Countries which have legislation in place focus primarily on assessment of risks for consumer health. Countries which have regulatory provisions for GM foods usually also regulate GMOs in general, taking into account health and environmental risks, as well as control- and trade-related issues (such as potential testing and labelling regimes). In view of the dynamics of the debate on GM foods, legislation is likely to continue to evolve.

10. What kind of GM foods are on the market internationally?

GM crops available on the international market today have been designed using one of three basic traits: resistance to insect damage; resistance to viral infections; and tolerance towards certain herbicides. GM crops with higher nutrient content (e.g. soybeans increased oleic acid) have been also studied recently.

11. What happens when GM foods are traded internationally?

The Codex Alimentarius Commission (Codex) is the joint FAO/WHO intergovernmental body responsible for developing the standards, codes of practice, guidelines and recommendations that constitute the Codex Alimentarius, meaning the international food code. Codex developed principles for the human health risk analysis of GM foods in 2003.

- Principles for the risk analysis of foods derived from modern biotechnology

    The premise of these principles sets out a premarket assessment, performed on a case-by-case basis and including an evaluation of both direct effects (from the inserted gene) and unintended effects (that may arise as a consequence of insertion of the new gene) Codex also developed three Guidelines:
- Guideline for the conduct of food safety assessment of foods derived from recombinant-DNA plants
- Guideline for the conduct of food safety assessment of foods produced using recombinant-DNA microorganisms
- Guideline for the conduct of food safety assessment of foods derived from recombinant-DNA animals

Codex principles do not have a binding effect on national legislation, but are referred to specifically in the Agreement on the Application of Sanitary and Phytosanitary Measures of the World Trade Organization (SPS Agreement), and WTO Members are encouraged to harmonize national standards with Codex standards. If trading partners have the same or similar mechanisms for the safety assessment of GM foods, the possibility that one product is approved in one country but rejected in another becomes smaller.

The Cartagena Protocol on Biosafety, an environmental treaty legally binding for its Parties which took effect in 2003, regulates transboundary movements of Living Modified Organisms (LMOs). GM foods are within the scope of the Protocol only if they contain LMOs that are capable of transferring or replicating genetic material. The cornerstone of the Protocol is a requirement that exporters seek consent from importers before the first shipment of LMOs intended for release into the environment.

12. Have GM products on the international market passed a safety assessment?

The GM products that are currently on the international market have all passed safety assessments conducted by national authorities. These different assessments in general follow the same basic principles, including an assessment of environmental and human health risk. The food safety assessment is usually based on Codex documents.

13. Why has there been concern about GM foods among some politicians, public interest groups and consumers?

Since the first introduction on the market in the mid-1990s of a major GM food (herbicide-resistant soybeans), there has been concern about such food among politicians, activists and consumers, especially in Europe. Several factors are involved. In the late 1980s–early 1990s, the results of decades of molecular research reached the public domain. Until that time, consumers were generally not very aware of the potential of this research. In the case of food, consumers started to wonder about safety because they perceive that modern biotechnology is leading to the creation of new species.

Consumers frequently ask, "what is in it for me?" Where medicines are concerned, many consumers more readily accept biotechnology as beneficial for their health (e.g. vaccines, medicines with improved treatment potential or increased safety). In the case of the first GM foods introduced onto the European market, the products were of no apparent direct benefit to consumers (not significantly cheaper, no increased shelflife, no better taste). The potential for GM seeds to result in bigger yields per cultivated area should lead to lower prices. However, public attention has focused on the risk side of the risk-benefit equation, often without distinguishing between potential environmental impacts and public health effects of GMOs.

Consumer confidence in the safety of food supplies in Europe has decreased significantly as a result of a number of food scares that took place in the second half of the 1990s that are unrelated to GM foods. This has also had an impact on discussions about the acceptability of GM foods. Consumers have questioned the validity of risk assessments, both with regard to consumer health and environmental risks, focusing in particular on long-term effects. Other topics debated by consumer organizations have included allergenicity and antimicrobial resistance. Consumer concerns have triggered a discussion on the desirability of labelling GM foods, allowing for an informed choice of consumers.

14. What is the state of public debate on GMOs?

The release of GMOs into the environment and the marketing of GM foods have resulted in a public debate in many parts of the world. This debate is likely to continue, probably in the broader context of other uses of biotechnology (e.g. in human medicine) and their consequences for human societies. Even though the issues under debate are usually very similar (costs and benefits, safety issues), the outcome of the debate differs from country to country. On issues such as labelling and traceability of GM foods as a way to address consumer preferences, there is no worldwide consensus to date. Despite the lack of consensus on these topics, the Codex Alimentarius Commission has made significant progress and developed Codex texts relevant to labelling of foods derived from modern biotechnology in 2011 to ensure consistency on any approach on labelling implemented by Codex members with already adopted Codex provisions.

15. Are people's reactions related to the different attitudes to food in various regions of the world?

Depending on the region of the world, people often have different attitudes to food. In addition to nutritional value, food often has societal and historical connotations, and in some instances may have religious importance. Technological modification of food and food production may evoke a negative response among consumers, especially in the absence of sound risk communication on risk assessment efforts and cost/benefit evaluations.

16. Are there implications for the rights of farmers to own their crops?

Yes, intellectual property rights are likely to be an element in the debate on GM foods, with an impact on the rights of farmers. In the FAO/WHO expert consultation in 2003 (http://www.who.int/entity/foodsafety/biotech/meetings/en/gmanimal_reportnov03_en.pdf), WHO and FAO have considered potential problems of the technological divide and the unbalanced distribution of benefits and risks between developed and developing countries and the problem often becomes even more acute through the existence of intellectual property rights and patenting that places an advantage on the strongholds of scientific and technological expertise. Such considerations are likely to also affect the debate on GM foods.

17. Why are certain groups concerned about the growing influence of the chemical industry on agriculture?

Certain groups are concerned about what they consider to be an undesirable level of control of seed markets by a few chemical companies. Sustainable agriculture and biodiversity benefit most from the use of a rich variety of crops, both in terms of good crop protection practices as well as from the perspective of society at large and the values attached to food. These groups fear that as a result of the interest of the chemical industry in seed markets, the range of varieties used by farmers may be reduced mainly to GM crops. This would impact on the food basket of a society as well as in the long run on crop protection (for example, with the development of resistance against insect pests and tolerance of certain herbicides). The exclusive use of herbicide-tolerant GM crops would also make the farmer dependent on these chemicals. These groups fear a dominant position of the chemical industry in agricultural development, a trend which they do not consider to be sustainable.

18. What further developments can be expected in the area of GMOs?

Future GM organisms are likely to include plants with improved resistance against plant disease or drought, crops with increased nutrient levels, fish species with enhanced growth characteristics. For non-food use, they may include plants or animals producing pharmaceutically important proteins such as new vaccines.

19. What has WHO been doing to improve the evaluation of GM foods?

WHO has been taking an active role in relation to GM foods, primarily for two reasons:

- on the grounds that public health could benefit from the potential of biotechnology, for example, from an increase in the nutrient content of foods, decreased allergenicity and more efficient and/or sustainable food production; and
- based on the need to examine the potential negative effects on human health of the consumption of food produced through genetic modification in order to protect public health. Modern technologies should be thoroughly evaluated if they are to constitute a true improvement in the way food is produced.

WHO, together with FAO, has convened several expert consultations on the evaluation of GM foods and provided technical advice for the Codex Alimentarius Commission which was fed into the Codex Guidelines on safety assessment of GM foods. WHO will keep paying due attention to the safety of GM foods from the view of public health protection, in close collaboration with FAO and other international bodies.

Genetically Modifying Plants Can Save Endangered Species

Muhammad Nakhooda

Muhammad Nakhooda is a senior lecturer in biotechnology at Cape Peninsula University of Technology in South Africa.

As the human population swells—and in the face of a changing and unpredictable climate—the demand for natural resources increases. This leads to distressing rates of deforestation to prepare land for agriculture, medicinal and forestry products. Related to this is an alarming reduction in species worldwide.

This can only be ameliorated through urgent, intensive and sustainable agroforestry and conservation initiatives. This involves the conservation of natural forests as well as renewable plantation efforts. But to date only a scattering of such projects are in place worldwide.

Conservation and renewable plantation efforts are trailing behind the rate of resource exploitation and species disappearance. The problem is worsened by the vast number of endangered plant species. Once disturbed from their natural habitat, they can't easily be reintroduced. This is because many of them do not readily produce seeds, or their seeds cannot be stored to ensure longevity of the species. The result is a decreasing gene pool.

This poses further risks, as vulnerable species become marginalised. They are only suitable to shrinking ranges and more susceptible to disease. To intensify conservation while enhancing agroforestry, smarter plant breeding practices are required.

"How Science Can Genetically Strengthen Endangered Plants and Agriculture," Muhammad Nakhooda, The Conversation, June 23, 2016. https://theconversation.com/how-science-can-genetically-strengthen-endangered-plants-and-agriculture-60468. Licensed under CC BY ND 4.0 International.

Traditional breeding has allowed for the identification, selection and propagation of plants with a superior genetic makeup, or genotype, from a given plant population. But traditional methods often fail to isolate the required superior characteristics of a species. They can also take more than five or six breeding cycles before a valuable trait is established and maintained in a plant population. The process can take decades for perennial plants, like trees.

Plant biotechnology is increasingly being used to complement traditional screening and breeding practices. Plants can be grown in test tubes under controlled laboratory conditions. Advances in biochemistry and genetics have also ushered in an understanding of the factors that influence plant growth.

Together these developments have created the opportunity to precisely identify and mass propagate superior plant varieties within a fraction of the time of traditional methods. On top of this, if required, the precise altering of the genetic makeup of plants is now also possible. This enables plant genomes to be radically enhanced so that superior genotypes can be created, maintained and propagated.

Preserving valuable genes

Maintaining superior genetics for valuable traits is fundamental in agroforestry. But to maintain superior genetics, seed production is rarely an option. In producing a seed, the sexual cross between genetically different male and female parent plants results in the dilution of valuable genes. This often leads to offspring with unpredictable genetics.

For the agroforestry industry to succeed, genotypes with predictably fast growth rates, high yields, and disease and drought resistance are needed. This will ensure land-use efficiency is maximised, which in turn will decrease ecological disturbance and protect indigenous plant species and sensitive natural forests.

One method that holds promise for preserving valuable genes is somatic embryogenesis. This is the ability to produce viable embryos from virtually any plant organ, while avoiding sexual crossing. Such embryos, when encased in alginate gel, constitute a synthetic seed. They retain all the valuable properties of the cloned parent plant.

Creating synthetic seeds

Somatic embryos may form naturally in certain plants, but can potentially be induced in any plant species and from any plant organ outside its normal biological context. This is done by altering the balance of plant hormones—the language signal in plants that controls all developmental processes.

Our research investigated the potential of inducing somatic embryos from leaves of the commercially important Eucalyptus tree. These are an important source of global timber products. Intensive efforts are under way to screen and select preferred genotypes to support environmental sustainability.

Somatic embryos mimic seeds without the lengthy breeding cycle. The germinated products are essentially clones of the parent plant from which the embryos were induced. So somatic embryogenesis allows for superior genotypes to be preserved. It also allows for the propagation of plant species that were previously excluded from standard propagation practices like traditional plant breeding or plant tissue culture.

There are other benefits too. The easily transported embryos constitute known genetics and growth properties. They could also potentially be cryopreserved, that is frozen to ultra-low temperatures indefinitely in liquid nitrogen. Importantly, because of the conditions under which they are induced, they are disease-free.

Despite its many uses somatic embryogenesis is only being used in selected agroforestry industries like sugarcane, certain conifer and forestry plantations and in a few ornamental plants. But its potential as a medium for genetic enhancement cannot be ignored, especially given recent advances in gene editing.

Gene editing

With the drive to sequence whole genomes of commercially important, rare or valuable plant species, scientists are presented with an opportunity to identify, understand the functions of and edit specific gene sequences to enhance plant properties.

To date, one hurdle to the success of the process has been the choice of organ when genetically editing plants.

This is why somatic embryos could be very useful for gene editing. As embryos they contain both root and shoot meristems—the precursors to a complete plant. If genes are edited at this embryonic stage, then as the embryo divides to form the complete plant all cells of the entire plant will carry the edited genome.

The advent of highly accurate gene editing methods has provided scientists with the opportunity to improve forestry, agricultural and threatened plant species. This can be done in a precise, targeted and reproducible manner. One such example is the Crispr/Cas9 system. This is a highly specific gene editing method that can be used to precisely replace whole gene sequences.

The potential exists to genetically insert tolerance to pests, disease, drought, floods and other pressures of a changing climate. Such precise gene editing will greatly benefit from readily available, disease-free embryos. In the near future, gene editing of synthetic seeds will allow extensive improvement of agricultural and forestry crops.

Planning for the future

The only historical limitation of somatic embryogenesis lay in the possibility of unplanned mutations arising from the embryo induction process. But advanced molecular screening techniques have mitigated this.

In time, we should expect to see greater use of enhanced, tolerant plant genotypes through specific gene editing of somatic embryos and synthetic seeds. What remains to be done is fervent research into the underlying mechanisms of somatic embryogenesis, their efficient conversion into synthetic seeds and successful cryopreservation. This should be done using a greater number of plant species for more efficient, productive, tolerant and sustainable agroforestry plantations, and in conservation programmes.

Genetically Modified Crops Are Increasing in the US with Positive Results

Jorge Fernandez-Cornejo, Seth J. Wechsler, and Michael Livingston

Jorge Fernandez-Cornejo, Seth J. Wechsler, and Michael Livingston are economists in the Structure, Technology and Productivity Branch in the Resource and Rural Economics Division of the US Department of Agriculture.

Genetically engineered (GE) crops with pest management traits first became commercially available for major crops in 1996. More than 15 years later, adoption of these crop varieties by U.S. farmers is widespread (170 million acres planted in 2013), and many products derived from these GE crops—including cornmeal, oils, and sugars—are commonly used in food products. While some GE seeds with traits that affect a crop's nutritional content and agronomic properties are already being commercialized and many more GE seeds are under development and testing, nearly all the GE seeds marketed to date to U.S. farmers are for pest management (pests here are defined to include insects, weeds, and some other organisms that interfere with the production of crops). Herbicide-tolerant (HT) seeds allow farmers to use certain effective herbicides to control weeds without damaging their crop. Other GE seeds leverage pesticidal proteins, naturally produced by the soil bacterium *Bacillus thuringiensis* (Bt), that are toxic to certain insects, protecting the plant over its entire life.

U.S. farmers tend to adopt HT seeds more than seeds with insect resistance partly because weeds are a pervasive problem. HT adoption was particularly rapid in soybeans, with U.S. farmers planting HT soybeans on 93 percent of all soybean acreage in

"Adoption of Genetically Engineered Crops by U.S. Farmers Has Increased Steadily for Over 15 Years," Jorge Fernandez-Cornejo, Seth J. Wechsler, and Michael Livingston, United States Department of Agriculture Economic Research Service, March 4, 2014.

2013. HT cotton occupied 82 percent of cotton acreage and HT corn 85 percent of corn acreage in 2013. Insect infestations tend to be more localized than weed infestations. Farmers planted Bt cotton (engineered to control insects such as tobacco budworm, bollworm, and pink bollworm) on 75 percent of cotton acreage in 2013. Bt corn—which controls the European corn borer, the corn rootworm, and the corn earworm—was planted on 76 percent of corn acres in 2013.

While corn, cotton, and soybeans account for the vast majority of GE acreage in the U.S., other GE crops commercially grown include HT canola, HT sugar beets, HT alfalfa, virus-resistant papaya, and virus-resistant squash. Since being commercially introduced, the varieties of GE seeds commercially available with pest management traits have increased in complexity, incorporating resistance to a broader range of insects and tolerance to more herbicides, as well as combining (or "stacking") both HT and Bt traits. With these innovations, the price of GE seeds increased, both in nominal and real terms. The rapid adoption of GE varieties by farmers is consistent with the belief that GE seeds provide improved performance or other benefits that make their use worthwhile, but what do research findings suggest?

GE seeds and yield losses to pests

In the absence of pests, commercially available GE seeds do not increase maximum crop yields. However, by protecting a plant from certain pests, GE crops can prevent yield losses to pests, allowing the plant to approach its yield potential. Bt crops are particularly effective at mitigating yield losses.

Average Bt corn yields have increased as new insect resistance traits have been incorporated into the seeds and seeds with multiple (stacked) traits have become available. In 1996, Bt corn was only resistant to one type of pest: the European corn borer. Since then, Bt corn resistance to corn rootworms (2003) and corn earworms (2010) has been introduced. Most experimental field tests and farm surveys show that Bt crops produce higher average yields than conventional crops. Data from USDA's Agricultural Resource Management Survey (ARMS) show that Bt corn yields were 17 bushels per acre higher than conventional corn yields in 2005 and about 26 bushels higher in 2010. Moreover, using an econometric model that controls for other factors, ERS researchers found that a 10-percent increase in the rate of Bt corn adoption was associated with a 1.7-percent increase in yields in 2005 and a 2.3-percent increase in yields in 2010. Researchers also found that a 10-percent increase in the adoption of Bt cotton in 1997 was associated with a 2.1-percent increase in yields.

On the other hand, evidence on the impact of HT seeds on soybean, corn, and cotton yields is mixed. Some researchers found no significant difference between the yields of adopters and non-adopters of HT; others found that HT adopters had higher yields, while still others found that adopters had lower yields.

An analysis of ARMS corn data indicates that stacked seeds (seeds with several GE traits) have higher yields than conventional seeds or seeds with only one GE trait. For example, 2010 ARMS data show that conventional corn seeds had an average yield of 134 bushels per acre. By contrast, seeds with two types of herbicide tolerance (glyphosate and glufosinate) and three types of insect resistance (corn borer, corn rootworm, and corn earworm) had an average yield of 171 bushels per acre.

Not surprisingly, adoption rates of stacked-seed varieties have increased quickly. Use of stacked corn seed grew from 1 percent of planted acres in 2000 to 71 percent in 2013. GE varieties incorporating three or four traits are now common.

Bt seeds, net returns, and household income

The market price of seed incorporates the costs associated with seed development, production, marketing, and distribution. The price of GE soybean and corn seeds grew by about 50 percent in real terms (adjusted for inflation) between 2001 and 2010. The price of GE cotton seed grew even faster. The increase in GE seed prices can be attributed in part to increasing price premiums over conventional seeds associated with the rising share of GE seeds with multiple (stacked) traits and /or more than one mode of action for particular target pests Another factor contributing to the increase in seed prices is the improvement in seed genetics (germplasm).

The profitability of GE seeds for individual farmers depends largely on the value of the yield losses mitigated and the pesticide and seed costs, which vary by crop and technology. Most studies show that adoption of Bt cotton and Bt corn is associated with increased net returns/variable profits. However, some studies of Bt corn show that profitability is strongly dependent on pest infestation levels (adoption of Bt cotton and Bt corn was associated with increased returns when the pest pressure was high).

The evidence on the impact of HT seeds on net returns is less consistent. Several researchers found that the adoption of herbicide-tolerant cotton had a positive impact on net returns. However, other researchers found no significant difference between the net returns of adopters and non-adopters of HT soybeans, and others found that HT soybean farmers are less profitable than their conventional counterparts. Overall, the empirical evidence on the impact of adopting herbicide-tolerant soybeans on net returns is inconclusive.

The fact that adoption of HT crops has been continuously rising, even though several researchers found no significant differences between the net returns of adopters and non-adopters, suggests that adopters derive other benefits. In particular, weed control for HT soybeans may be simpler and more flexible (e.g., HT seed-based production programs allow growers to use one product to control a wide range of both broadleaf and grass weeds instead of using several herbicides to achieve adequate weed control), freeing up valuable management time for leisure, or to generate enterprise growth or off-farm income.

ERS research shows that HT adoption is associated with increased off-farm household income for U.S. soybean farmers, most likely because time savings associated with HT crops were used in off-farm employment. More recently, other researchers confirmed that GE crops led to household labor savings and that farmers adopting GE crops derived value from the convenience, flexibility, and increased worker safety associated with growing HT crops that enable them to use fewer toxic herbicides.

Adoption and pesticide use

Studies based on field tests and farm surveys have examined the extent to which GE crop adoption affects pesticide (insecticide and herbicide) use, and most results show a reduction in pesticide use. A 2010 National Research Council study concurred that GE crops lead to reduced pesticide use and /or to use of pesticides with lower toxicity compared to those used on conventional crops.

Generally, Bt adoption is associated with lower levels of insecticide use. Pounds of insecticide (per planted acre) applied to corn and cotton crops have decreased steadily over the last 10 years (except for cotton in 1999-2001, when application levels were distorted during the boll weevil eradication program).

Insecticide use trends suggest that insect infestation levels on corn and cotton farms were lower in 2010 than in earlier years and are consistent with the fact that European corn borer populations have steadily declined over the last decade. In addition, several researchers have shown that areawide suppression of certain insects such as the European corn borer and the pink bollworm are associated with Bt corn and Bt cotton use, respectively. This suggests that Bt seeds have benefited not only adopters but non-adopters as well.

Herbicide use on corn, cotton and soybean acres (measured in pounds per planted acre) declined slightly in the first years following introduction of HT seeds in 1996, but increased modestly in later years. Despite the relatively minor effect HT crop adoption has had on overall herbicide usage, HT crop adoption has enabled farmers to substitute glyphosate (which many HT crops are designed to tolerate) for more traditional herbicides. Because glyphosate is significantly less toxic and less persistent than traditional herbicides, the net impact of HT crop adoption is an improvement in environmental quality and a reduction in health risks.

HT crops and conservation tillage

Conservation tillage (including no-till, ridge-till, and mulch-till) is known to provide environmental benefits and is facilitated by use of HT crops. By leaving at least 30 percent of crop residue covering the soil surface after all the tillage and planting operations, conservation tillage reduces soil erosion by wind and water, increases water retention, and reduces soil degradation and water/chemical runoff. In addition, conservation tillage reduces the carbon footprint of agriculture.

By 2006, approximately 86 percent of HT soybean planted acres were under conservation tillage, compared to only 36 percent of conventional soybean acres. Differences in the use of no-till were just as pronounced. While approximately 45 percent of HT soybean acres were cultivated using no-till technologies in 2006, only 5 percent of the acres planted with conventional seeds were cultivated using no-till techniques, which are often considered the most effective of all conservation tillage systems. Cotton and corn data exhibit similar though less pronounced patterns.

These trends suggest that HT crop adoption facilitates the use of conservation tillage practices. In addition, a review of several econometric studies points to a two-way causal relationship between the adoption of HT crops and conservation tillage. Thus, in addition to its direct effects on herbicide usage, adoption of herbicide-tolerant crops indirectly benefits the environment by encouraging the use of conservation tillage.

Future trends

The acceptance of GE crops by farmers has been due, in large part, to the pest management traits incorporated into GE seeds. Farmers were willing to adopt GE seeds because their benefits exceeded their costs, while domestic consumers were largely indifferent to these traits. But how long can farmers expect to benefit from the pest management traits engineered into the seeds currently commercially available? And, what other traits might be engineered into seeds that would attract farmer and consumer interest?

As with other efforts to control agricultural pests, pests will inevitably develop resistance to the pest management traits incorporated in GE seeds. Prior to the commercial introduction of Bt crops, entomologists and other scientists persuasively argued that mandatory minimum refuge requirements (planting sufficient acres of the non-Bt crop near the Bt crop) were needed to reduce the rate at which targeted insect pests evolved resistance. Analysis of more than a decade of monitoring data suggests that minimum refuge requirements and natural refuges have indeed helped delay the evolution of Bt resistance in some insect pests. However, Bt resistance in western corn rootworm, cotton bollworm, and fall armyworm populations leading to reduced efficacy of Bt corn and Bt cotton has been recently documented in some U.S. crop fields.

Likewise, an overreliance on glyphosate and a reduction in the diversity of weed management practices by HT crop producers contributed to the evolution of glyphosate resistance in 14 weed species in the United States. Because no new major classes of herbicides have been made commercially available in the last 20 years, and because few new ones are expected to be available soon, growing resistance to glyphosate is expected to reduce the benefit farmers derive from using the most widely available HT seed varieties. Furthermore, the weed management practices needed to slow the spread of glyphosate-resistant weeds may themselves reduce the short-term benefits of planting glyphosate-tolerant (i.e., HT) seeds. As a result, their benefits may erode over time in the absence of further developments affecting HT seeds and their associated herbicides and/or improvements in weed management practices. One such development is the introduction of crops tolerant to the herbicides dicamba and 2, 4-D if used in the context of a diversified approach to weed management.

While relatively few GE traits are currently commercially available, the number of field releases to test GE varieties approved by USDA's Animal and Plant Health Inspection Service indicates continued GE-related R&D activities since field testing is a critical part of seed development. The number of field releases grew from 4 in 1985 to 1,194 in 2002 and has since averaged around 800 per year. Other measures suggest that GE-related R&D activity has increased dramatically since 2005.

Field releases approved for GE varieties continue to focus heavily on herbicide tolerance and insect resistance, but other traits are being developed and tested in large numbers as well. These include traits that provide favorable agronomic properties (resistance to cold/drought/frost/salinity, more efficient use of nitrogen, increased yield); enhanced product quality, such as delayed ripening, flavor and texture (fruits and vegetables); increased protein or carbohydrate content, fatty acid content, or micronutrient content; modified starch, color (cotton, flowers), fiber properties (cotton), or gluten content (wheat); naturally decaffeinated (coffee); and nutraceuticals (added vitamins, iron, antioxidants such as beta-carotene).

New HT and insect resistance traits may give farmers more pest management options and slow the spread of pesticide resistance among pest populations. Approval of other "first generation" traits that improve yields or reduce yield losses could result in further adoption of GE varieties. Farmer response to the approval of "second generation" traits that alter end product quality may be more cautious. Farmers can expect to benefit from the adoption of these GE traits only if consumer acceptance is assured. In short, the future of GE seed use depends on the ability of farmers to adopt best management practices, the ability of biotech companies to develop new GE varieties, and consumer acceptance of products from GE sources.

GMO Foods Are Unsafe, Unhealthy, and Harm the Environment

Jeffrey Smith

Jeffrey Smith is the founder of the website Institute for Responsible Technology, which seeks to educate consumers about genetically modified foods and crops.

1. GMOs are unhealthy.

The American Academy of Environmental Medicine (AAEM) urges doctors to prescribe non-GMO diets for all patients. They cite animal studies showing organ damage, gastrointestinal and immune system disorders, accelerated aging, and infertility. Human studies show how genetically modified (GM) food can leave material behind inside us, possibly causing long-term problems. Genes inserted into GM soy, for example, can transfer into the DNA of bacteria living inside us, and that the toxic insecticide produced by GM corn was found in the blood of pregnant women and their unborn fetuses.

Numerous health problems increased after GMOs were introduced in 1996. The percentage of Americans with three or more chronic illnesses jumped from 7% to 13% in just 9 years; food allergies skyrocketed, and disorders such as autism, reproductive disorders, digestive problems, and others are on the rise. Although there is not sufficient research to confirm that GMOs are a contributing factor, doctors groups such as the AAEM tell us not to wait before we start protecting ourselves, and especially our children who are most at risk.

The American Public Health Association and American Nurses Association are among many medical groups that condemn the use of GM bovine growth hormone, because the milk from treated cows has more of the hormone IGF-1 (insulin-like growth factor 1)—which is linked to cancer.

"10 Reasons to Avoid GMOs," Jeffrey Smith, Institute for Responsible Technology, August 25, 2011. Reprinted by permission.

2. GMOs contaminate forever.

GMOs cross pollinate and their seeds can travel. It is impossible to fully clean up our contaminated gene pool. Self-propagating GMO pollution will outlast the effects of global warming and nuclear waste. The potential impact is huge, threatening the health of future generations. GMO contamination has also caused economic losses for organic and non-GMO farmers who often struggle to keep their crops pure.

3. GMOs increase herbicide use.

Most GM crops are engineered to be "herbicide tolerant"—they [resist] deadly weed killer. Monsanto, for example, sells Roundup Ready crops, designed to survive applications of their Roundup herbicide.

Between 1996 and 2008, US farmers sprayed an extra 383 million pounds of herbicide on GMOs. Overuse of Roundup results in "superweeds," resistant to the herbicide. This is causing farmers to use even more toxic herbicides every year. Not only does this create environmental harm, GM foods contain higher residues of toxic herbicides. Roundup, for example, is linked with sterility, hormone disruption, birth defects, and cancer.

4. Genetic engineering creates dangerous side effects.

By mixing genes from totally unrelated species, genetic engineering unleashes a host of unpredictable side effects. Moreover, irrespective of the type of genes that are inserted, the very process of creating a GM plant can result in massive collateral damage that produces new toxins, allergens, carcinogens, and nutritional deficiencies.

5. Government oversight is dangerously lax.

Most of the health and environmental risks of GMOs are ignored by governments' superficial regulations and safety assessments. The reason for this tragedy is largely political. The US Food and Drug

Administration (FDA), for example, doesn't require a single safety study, does not mandate labeling of GMOs, and allows companies to put their GM foods onto the market without even notifying the agency. Their justification was the claim that they had no information showing that GM foods were substantially different. But this was a lie. Secret agency memos made public by a lawsuit show that the overwhelming consensus even among the FDA's own scientists was that GMOs can create unpredictable, hard-to-detect side effects. They urged long-term safety studies. But the White House had instructed the FDA to promote biotechnology, and the agency official in charge of policy was Michael Taylor, Monsanto's former attorney, later their vice president. He's now the US Food Safety Czar.

6. The biotech industry uses "tobacco science" to claim product safety.

Biotech companies like Monsanto told us that Agent Orange, PCBs, and DDT were safe. They are now using the same type of superficial, rigged research to try and convince us that GMOs are safe. Independent scientists, however, have caught the spin-masters red-handed, demonstrating without doubt how industry-funded research is designed to avoid finding problems, and how adverse findings are distorted or denied.

7. Independent research and reporting is attacked and suppressed.

Scientists who discover problems with GMOs have been attacked, gagged, fired, threatened, and denied funding. The journal Nature acknowledged that a "large block of scientists . . . denigrate research by other legitimate scientists in a knee-jerk, partisan, emotional way that is not helpful in advancing knowledge." Attempts by media to expose problems are also often censored.

8. GMOs harm the environment.

GM crops and their associated herbicides can harm birds, insects, amphibians, marine ecosystems, and soil organisms. They reduce bio-diversity, pollute water resources, and are unsustainable. For example, GM crops are eliminating habitat for monarch butterflies, whose populations are down 50% in the US. Roundup herbicide has been shown to cause birth defects in amphibians, embryonic deaths and endocrine disruptions, and organ damage in animals even at very low doses. GM canola has been found growing wild in North Dakota and California, threatening to pass on its herbicide tolerant genes on to weeds.

9. GMOs do not increase yields, and work against feeding a hungry world.

Whereas sustainable non-GMO agricultural methods used in developing countries have conclusively resulted in yield increases of 79% and higher, GMOs do not, on average, increase yields at all. This was evident in the Union of Concerned Scientists' 2009 report Failure to Yield—the definitive study to date on GM crops and yield.

The International Assessment of Agricultural Knowledge, Science and Technology for Development (IAASTD) report, authored by more than 400 scientists and backed by 58 governments, stated that GM crop yields were "highly variable" and in some cases, "yields declined." The report noted, "Assessment of the technology lags behind its development, information is anecdotal and contradictory, and uncertainty about possible benefits and damage is unavoidable." They determined that the current GMOs have nothing to offer the goals of reducing hunger and poverty, improving nutrition, health and rural livelihoods, and facilitating social and environmental sustainability.

On the contrary, GMOs divert money and resources that would otherwise be spent on more safe, reliable, and appropriate technologies.

10. By avoiding GMOs, you contribute to the coming tipping point of consumer rejection, forcing them out of our food supply.

Because GMOs give no consumer benefits, if even a small percentage of us start rejecting brands that contain them, GM ingredients will become a marketing liability. Food companies will kick them out. In Europe, for example, the tipping point was achieved in 1999, just after a high profile GMO safety scandal hit the papers and alerted citizens to the potential dangers. In the US, a consumer rebellion against GM bovine growth hormone has also reached a tipping point, kicked the cow drug out of dairy products by Wal-Mart, Starbucks, Dannon, Yoplait, and most of America's dairies.

Genetically Modified Foods Pose Ethical Questions

Christopher Mayes

Christopher Mayes is a postdoctoral research fellow at the Centre for Values, Ethics and the Law in Medicine at the University of Sydney. His latest book is The Biopolitics of Lifestyle: Foucault, Ethics and Health Choices.

Food is cultural, social and deeply personal, so it's no surprise that modifications to the way food is produced, distributed and consumed often lead to ethical debates.

Developments in the genetic modification (GM) of foods and crops has resulted in a raft of controversies.

Ethics can help here. While science determines whether we can safely modify the genetic makeup of certain organisms, ethics asks whether we should.

Ethics tries to move beyond factual statements about what is, to evaluative statements about the way we *should* act towards ourselves, each other and the environment we inhabit. But things are not always so clear-cut.

Three areas of ethics can help frame some of the concerns with GM food and crops: virtue, moral status and consequences.

Virtues vs vices

Ethics of GM foods can be developed by looking at virtue or character. Does the activity of engaging in the development of GM foods and crops erode virtues while producing vices? Or is GM technology a prudent use of knowledge for humanitarian goals?

"Because We Can, Does It Mean We Should: The Ethics of GM Foods," Christopher Mayes, The Conversation, June 26, 2014. https://theconversation.com/because-we-can-does-it-mean-we-should-the-ethics-of-gm-foods-28141. Licensed under CC BY ND 4.0 International.

Character or virtue-based arguments are seen in the case of golden rice—a rice strain modified to contain beta-carotene, a precursor of vitamin A.

According to the World Health Organisation more than 250 million preschool age children are vitamin A deficient (VAD), and two million deaths and more than half a million cases of blindness are attributed to VAD. The developers of golden rice say it will supply 60% of the recommended daily intake of vitamin A.

But global outrage ensued after group of Filipino farmers destroyed a test crop of golden rice. There has been little recognition of the Sisyphean struggle of farmers in countries such as the Philippines, Bangladesh and India, yet these farmers have been described as anti-science Luddites and contributing to the deaths of children.

Critics of golden rice such as Wendell Berry and Vandana Shiva argue that GM technology is a solution offered by industrial agriculture to address problems created by industrial agriculture.

Golden rice is a techno-scientific fix to structural problems created by some of the very companies that may profit from GM crops.

Although golden rice is a non-profit initiative, Shiva argues that it is a trojan horse to give GM crops a humanitarian face.

According to opponents such as Shiva, golden rice and GM crops not only pose negative consequences for farmers, environment and the global poor, but represent vices of greed, arrogance and dominance. Rather than humbly working with and caring for the natural environment, industrial and technological interventions seek to master, profit and control.

Morality of nature

There are also concerns about the moral status of the organism itself—does the modification of an organism's genetic makeup represent a wrong to the dignity or integrity to the organism?

This position depends on arguments that nature has dignity and interests beyond those of its human inhabitants. Such arguments are not readily accepted due to their metaphysical or theological overtones and dependence on essentialist idea of nature.

Appeals to nature can led to what British philosopher G.E. Moore described as the naturalistic fallacy—the idea that we can derive moral statements from facts of nature. Examples include:

- raw milk is good because it's natural
- standing desks are good because we weren't meant to sit
- genetically modified crops are wrong because they're unnatural.

Perhaps we aren't so concerned about the essential dignity of rice or wheat, but what about GM pigs that glow in the dark, featherless chickens, cows that produce human milk or the integrity of an ecosystem? Although the arguments are relatively the same, in discussing GM animals, the idea of a natural integrity or dignity seems more compelling.

Weighing up consequences

The most common way of framing the ethics of GM foods is to ask: do GM foods and crops present negative or harmful consequences for individuals, populations or the environment? Answers to this question vary according to context.

Most scientists argue that GM foods are safe to eat and will not harm consumer health.

While critics maintain that long-term health effects are uncertain, they contend that even if GM foods are safe to eat other harmful consequences should be considered, such as the impact of patenting lawson farmers and research integrity, or the risk of GM crops contaminatingother crops or escaping into the wild.

Debates over consequences tend to avoid the question of whether there is something inherently objectionable about GM foods and crops. So long as there is appropriate management of risks, then theoretically, there is no ethical problem.

It is unlikely these issues will be resolved any time soon—and likely that new ones will be added—but one area that can be worked on is discourse ethics.

Describing opponents of golden rice, even those that destroy test crops, as committing crimes against humanity or those in favour as pursing economic self-interest does little to move the debate forward.

Until productive discourse is established, barriers between opposing views will only strengthen.

CHAPTER 4

Is the Genetic Engineering of Animals Ethical?

Overview: Animals Are Genetically Engineered for a Variety of Purposes and Are Closely Regulated

US Food and Drug Administration

The US Food and Drug Administration is the federal agency that protects public health by assuring that foods are safe, wholesome, sanitary, and properly labeled.

Q: *What is genetic engineering?*
A: Genetic engineering generally refers to the use of tools of modern biotechnology and molecular biology to introduce new genetic material, or delete or alter existing genetic material to introduce intended, new traits or characteristics.

Q: *What is a genetically engineered animal?*
A: A genetically engineered (GE) animal is one that contains additional or altered genetic material (e.g., recombinant DNA (rDNA)) through use of modern biotechnology tools that's intended to give the animal a new trait or characteristic. Examples of the kind of GE animals that are being developed are provided below.

Q: *What kinds of GE animals are being developed?*
A: Many kinds of GE animals are in development.

- *Biopharm* animals are those that have undergone genetic engineering to produce particular substances, such as human insulin, for pharmaceutical use.
- *Research* animals may be engineered to make them more susceptible to particular diseases, such as cancer, in order to gain a better basic understanding of the disease for the development of new therapies or in order to evaluate new medical therapies.

"Consumer Q & A," US Food and Drug Administration.

- *Xenotransplant* animals are being engineered so they can be used as sources for cells, tissues or organs that can be used for transplantation into humans.
- *Companion* animals that are modified to enrich or enhance their interaction with humans (i.e., hypoallergenic pets).
- *Disease resistant* animals may be used either for food use or biopharm applications. These animals have received modifications that make them resistant to common diseases, such as mastitis (a very painful infection of the udder) in dairy cows, or particularly deadly diseases, such as bovine spongiform encephalopathy (BSE).
- *Food use* animals have been engineered to provide healthier meat, such as pigs that contain healthy omega-3 fatty acids at levels comparable to those in fish.

Q: How are GE animals regulated?

A: FDA regulates GE animals under the "new animal drug" [The new animal drug approval requirements are described in the Code of Federal Regulations under 21 CFR 514.] provisions of the Federal Food, Drug, and Cosmetic Act (FD&C Act) and FDA's implementing regulations for new animal drugs. This guidance is intended to help industry understand the requirements that are established by statute and regulations as they apply to these animals, including those of the National Environmental Policy Act (NEPA), and to inform the public about the process FDA is using to regulate GE animals. The guidance does not create any new obligations. It clarifies how the regulations apply to GE animals.

Q: What's the difference between animal clones and GE animals?

A: The animal clones that were the subject of FDA's risk assessment on animal cloning (released in January of 2008) are "just clones"—that is, they are copies of individual conventionally-bred animals, and do not contain any rDNA constructs. What can be confusing is that an animal clone can be genetically engineered (i.e., have an rDNA construct introduced into it), and a GE animal can be reproduced by cloning. Our guidance covers GE animals, irrespective of whether they were reproduced by cloning. It does not cover animal clones that do not contain an rDNA construct ("just clones").

Q: Why is FDA regulating GE animals differently from animal clones?

A: Clones are really just genetic copies of the animals from which they are produced. The purpose of the FDA risk assessment was to determine whether cloning posed any new risks to the health of animals and whether animal clones posed new food safety risks. The conclusion of that risk assessment was that there are no new risks associated with those animals, that food from cattle, swine, and goat clones, and the progeny of the clone of any species traditionally consumed as food was as safe to eat as that from conventionally bred animals, and that no new regulatory requirements are necessary beyond those that apply to other, conventionally-bred animals. By contrast, GE animals have changes to their genetic material that may potentially affect the health of the GE animal or the safety of food from the GE animal. Therefore, there are risk-based reasons for FDA to require their approval.

Q: Will GE animals be regulated the same if they're used for food or if they're intended to produce pharmaceuticals for people?

A: GE animals are subject to premarket oversight whether they are intended to be used for food or to produce pharmaceuticals or other useful products. There may be some differences in what the actual oversight process entails depending on the kinds of risk(s) the GE animals may pose, and the kinds of uses for which they are intended. In addition, the pharmaceuticals produced from GE animals must be approved through the same process as applies to other pharmaceuticals. In general, we do not anticipate that biopharm animals will be used for food.

Q: What kind of post-market surveillance will there be?

A: Post-market surveillance will vary depending on the GE animal. However, as with conventional new animal drugs, the guidance tells sponsors (individuals or companies submitting GE animal applications to FDA for review) that in their application they should demonstrate that the rDNA construct is stable in the animal over time, and that the GE animal retains the new characteristics over time. As with conventional drugs, if additional information shows that there are safety concerns, or if the GE animal no longer has the characteristics claimed for it, FDA can take steps to have the GE animal removed from the market.

Q: Will FDA be looking at effects on the health of animals?

A: Before FDA can approve a new animal drug, it must determine that the drug is safe for the animal receiving it. Therefore, before we can approve a GE animal, we must determine that the rDNA construct is safe for the animal containing it. To do that, we look at the health of the animal. In the guidance, we provide recommendations on how developers can assess the health of their animals.

Q: Is food from GE animals in the food supply?

A: On November 19, 2015, FDA approved an application related to AquAdvantage Salmon, a GE Atlantic salmon. Although these salmon will be bred in Canada, and raised in Panama, food from these salmon will be imported into the U.S. For details on the kinds of studies that were conducted to assess food safety, please see the Freedom of Information Summary, Section IX.

We will not approve any GE animal for food use unless we find that the food from those GE animals is safe. It would be illegal to introduce food from an unapproved GE animal into the food supply without FDA permission. We work closely with GE animal producers to make sure that they keep good records of their animals and that none enter the food supply without FDA approval.

Q: Will food from GE animals be labeled?

A: The FDA recognizes that many consumers are interested in whether food ingredients are derived from genetically engineered plants or animals, and is also publishing guidance for manufacturers who wish to voluntarily label their foods as containing or not containing such ingredients. If food from a GE animal is materially different from its non-engineered counterpart (for example, if it has a different nutritional profile), the difference would be material information that would have to be indicated in the labeling. Marketers may voluntarily label their foods as coming from GE or non-GE animals, as long as the labeling is truthful and not misleading. FDA oversees labeling of most fish and seafood, of milk and other dairy products, and of whole eggs in their shells. The U. S. Department of Agriculture's Food Safety and Inspection Service (FSIS) generally oversees labels used for meat, poultry, and other egg products.

Q: Will GE animals be labeled?

A: Developers of GE animals will need to have labeling accompanying the animals. The guidance recommends that the labeling describe the GE animal (e.g., common name/breed/line, genus, species, GE animal line, rDNA construct), and its intended use. Where the labeling for a GE animal contains animal care or safety information (e.g., husbandry or containment), we recommend that the labeling accompany the animal throughout all stages of its lifecycle.

Q: What other agencies are involved in the regulation of these animals?

A: Depending on the species and use of the animal in question, the U.S. Department of Agriculture's Animal and Plant Health Inspection Service (APHIS), FSIS, the Environmental Protection Agency, and others may play a role in the regulation of GE animals. FDA is working very closely with these agencies and Departments to coordinate the regulation of these animals.

Q: What about environmental effects?

A: Environmental evaluation that meets the requirements of NEPA is required prior to any approval. We expect that the environmental risks that may be posed by GE animals will differ on a case-by-case basis. For example, the concerns raised by a GE cow that is resistant to mastitis will be very different from the concerns raised by a GE fresh-water fish that is engineered to grow more rapidly. We will work closely with individual GE animal producers to make sure that their environmental assessments address all of the potential risks these animals may pose.

Q: Can food from biopharm animals be eaten?

A: In general, biopharm animals are not intended to be eaten: they are engineered to produce a therapeutic substance, and their value is in that product and not the meat or milk from the animal. Given the relatively small numbers of any particular line of biopharm animal, the large amount of food safety data that is required to be provided to FDA for each GE animal line intended to enter the food supply, and the kind of food safety issues that pharmaceutical chemicals present in such animals would generally pose, it would be very unusual for developers of biopharm animals to want to enter their animals into the food supply. Without FDA approval for food use, it would be illegal for a company to direct any of its GE animals into the food supply. It is much more likely that these animals will be disposed of in a way that does not involve human food use when they have reached the end of their lives.

However, if a developer provided sufficient evidence of safety and FDA approved the biopharm animal for food use, then the decision on whether to enter it into the food supply would be a marketing issue for the food producer and the developer and not a food safety issue.

Q: What are the potential benefits of GE animals for consumers?

A: Many GE animals in development are intended to have direct benefits to consumers. For instance, biopharm animals are being developed to produce various pharmaceuticals for humans or other animals such as clotting factors, growth factors and inhibitors used in cancer therapy, some of which cannot now be produced in sufficient quantities to meet medical needs. Some GE animals are under development to produce healthier food. And other animals are under development to have indirect benefits to consumers, such as decreased environmental impact by excreting lower levels of pollutants in their wastes.

Q: Are there any GE animals on the market now?
A: In 2003, FDA chose to exercise enforcement discretion for a GE aquarium fish that fluoresces in the dark. FDA made this decision in part because the fish (Zebra danio) is not a species used for food, and in part because the agency was able to determine that it did not pose any additional environmental risks compared with conventional Zebra danios. (Zebra danios are unable to survive outside the very warm waters of the tropics, which effectively limits the ability of an escaped or released fish to affect the U.S. environment.)

Additionally, there are many different kinds of GE rats and mice used in laboratory research throughout the world.

In addition, as described below, FDA has approved three GE animal-related applications. The first was in 2009, when FDA's Center for Veterinary Medicine approved a GE goat that produced a human biologic in its milk. The Center for Biologics Evaluation and Research approved the human biologic, ATryn. In November 2015, FDA approved an application related to AquAdvantage Salmon, a GE Atlantic salmon. In December 2015, FDA's Center for Veterinary Medicine approved a GE chicken that produces a human biologic in its eggs. The Center for Drug Evaluation and Research approved the human biologic, Kanuma (sebelipase alfa).

Q: How long have GE animals existed? Why did FDA step in when it did?
A: The first GE animal, a rabbit, was produced in the 1980s. Since that time, the field has grown enormously. FDA has been monitoring and evaluating the development of GE animals and

believes that it is important now to provide the growing industry with a clear and transparent regulatory path. We also think it's important to let other stakeholders, including the public, know our policies and requirements on this issue. Because we are a science-based public health agency, we are using a rigorous regulatory approach to ensure the public health, while providing GE animal developers a path by which they can bring innovative products to the market. In addition, the Codex Alimentarius, an international food safety standards organization sponsored by the United Nations, adopted a guideline on assessing the safety of food from GE animals. We therefore realized it was a good time to ensure that developers, both in the U.S. and around the world, understood what FDA's regulatory requirements are regarding GE animals and food from such animals.

Q: Do GE animals look different from other animals?
A: Despite some of the doctored photographs that you may have seen circulating on the internet, adding a new gene to an animal does not result in outlandish physical combinations, such as a bird with the head of a rabbit. Genetic engineering simply doesn't work that way.

Almost all GE animals will look the same as their conventional counterparts, although there are some products in which the point of the GE process is to make the animal look slightly different (such as the GloFish).

Q: Are the offspring of a GE animal also considered GE?
A: In general, most GE animals that are being developed at this time are intended to pass their new GE traits on to their offspring. Such traits are called heritable. The initial GE animal and all of its descendants that have inherited the GE trait are called GE animals. Other GE animals have "non-heritable" traits, meaning that none of the offspring will have the trait. This guidance deals only with GE animals bearing heritable traits.

Q: Is it possible that GE animals could displace or replace the conventional species?
A: Over time, it is at least theoretically possible that certain GE traits might be widely adopted. For example, were ducks and chickens developed that could not carry or transmit avian influenza, it is possible that many producers of such animals, particularly in vulnerable parts of the world, would want to introduce that trait throughout their flocks. Such a trend would be no different than what already has occurred with the popular conventional livestock breeds currently used in agriculture. Such widespread adoption of any particular GE trait would likely be quite unusual.

It also would be extremely unlikely for any GE animal to accidentally displace conventional animals. Most developers of the GE animals will likely control their breeding opportunities to further their business interests. For example, GE animals producing pharmaceutical products must be carefully confined in controlled conditions, such as limited access barns, to ensure that diseases or other contaminants do not make their way into the final pharmaceutical products.

Q: Is there a chance that this technology could be used on humans?
A: Gene therapy has been used to attempt to treat various human diseases since 1990, and is subject to strict FDA oversight under a process different from that described in this guidance. Human gene therapy is currently limited to non-heritable therapies; that is, people who receive the new genes as part of the gene therapy can't pass them on to their children. To date there have been no gene therapies approved for humans, although several clinical trials are ongoing.

Q: What exactly does the review process of a GE animal entail?
A: The guidance recommends a review process that includes seven categories:

- *Product definition:* a broad statement characterizing the GE animal and the claim being made for the GE animal;

- *Molecular characterization of the construct:* a description of the rDNA construct or other genomic alteration and how they are produced;
- *Molecular characterization of the GE animal lineage:* a description of the method by which the rDNA construct or other genomic alteration was introduced into the animal and whether they are stably maintained over time;
- *Phenotypic characterization of the GE animal:* comprehensive data on the characteristics of the GE animal and its health;
- *Durability plan:* the sponsor's plan to demonstrate that the alteration will remain the same over time, and continue to have the same effect;
- *Environmental and food/feed safety:* the assessment of any environmental impacts, and for GE animals of food species, an assessment of the safety of food derived from those GE animals is safe to eat for humans and/or animals;
- *Claim validation:* a demonstration that the GE animal has the characteristics that the developer says it has.

Q: *When will the first approvals be granted?*

A: FDA has approved three GE animal-related applications. The first was in 2009, when FDA's Center for Veterinary Medicine approved a GE goat that produced a human biologic in its milk. The Center for Biologics Evaluation and Research approved the human biologic, ATryn. In November 2015, FDA approved an application related to AquAdvantage Salmon, a GE Atlantic salmon. In December 2015, FDA's Center for Veterinary Medicine approved a GE chicken that produces a human biologic in its eggs. The Center for Drug Evaluation and Research approved the human biologic, Kanuma (sebelipase alfa). No additional applications for GE animals will be approved until FDA determines that the rDNA construct in the animals is safe for the animals and is effective, i.e., that the GE animals do indeed possess the traits that they were intended to express, and that, if the animals are intended to be used as food, the food is safe to eat. All approvals will be handled on a case-by-case basis, and as with any approval, it is difficult to estimate how long it will take to produce the data for the agency to evaluate, and when any one of those reviews will be completed.

Q. How will FDA inform the public about new GE animals, its decisions on them, and the science behind those decisions?
A. The agency is interested in increasing the transparency of its deliberations and actions. In particular, we intend to seek input from experts and the public where there is significant public interest in an issue, and FDA believes the public may have relevant data or information to contribute. Additionally, as is the case for all NADAs, after completion of an NADA, the agency will post a Freedom of Information summary of the information in the NADA file, including information used to assess safety (to the animal and for food or feed, if appropriate) and in support of the claims made by the sponsor.

We have developed a number of consumer-appropriate publications to help inform consumers and other stakeholders about the technology and the agency's regulations of these animals. These are available on the FDA website.

FDA's new animal drug approvals (including for GE animals) are published in the Federal Register, codified in the Code of Federal Regulations, and posted on its website at Animal Drugs @ FDA. Following approvals, FDA will also provide electronic access to a summary of all information (other than confidential business or trade secret information) used in FDA's decisions as part of the freedom of information summary routinely published upon approval.

Q: What about the ethics of genetically engineering animals?
A: The issue of ethics is an extremely complicated one. On the one hand, the standard for approval does not explicitly include ethics—FDA must regulate on the basis of safety and effectiveness. However, many people would consider animal health and safety to be a subcategory of the broader term "ethics." To that end, the regulatory approach described in this guidance closely examines

animal health and requires a finding of safety to animals, and so we believe that we are addressing those particular concerns.

We do, however, recognize that genetically engineering animals may raise non-scientific social concerns that may fall under the heading of "ethics." We note that these issues are not within the scope of the guidance. We do, however, continue to participate in various venues in which these issues are discussed so that we can ensure that the discussions are based on fact and not on erroneous assumptions regarding the technology or its outcomes.

Q: Where can I get more information about genetic engineering and the GE Guidance for Industry?

A: The Guidance for Industry is available on FDA's website.

Genetically Engineering Animals Can Provide High-Quality Food

Aaron Saenz

Aaron Saenz is a former senior editor at Singularity Hub, a news website that covers the technology industry.

I t's been more than a decade since humans have cracked their own genetic code, but we've yet to wake up to a world of engineered lifeforms on the Island of Dr. Moreau. While we're waiting for genetic science to mature maybe we should take a good long look at cows. Specifically, the Belgian Blue. This muscle bound meathead is a monument to the genetic power of selective breeding. A single genetic defect, a faulty myostatin gene, is responsible for its enormous bulk, and that defect was carefully passed on through the breed for more than a century before it was even known what was causing the cattle's impressive "double muscling." Watch the introduction to life of the modern Belgian Blue in [a] video from National Geographic. Before we dive into modifying the human gene pool, we better learn the lessons that working with the Belgian Blue has taught us: even the most primitive genetic tools are immensely powerful, they raise serious ethical concerns, and their results are so impressive as to almost guarantee their use. With genetic testing on the rise, and artificial insemination more prevalent, sex is primed to undergo a major renaissance in the years before it's outdone by genetic engineering.

For those who have never seen a Belgian Blue in person, the experience is...dramatic. Imagine walking past a dozen or so regular bulls and being intimidated by their sheer size and strength. Then imagine passing a bull so heavily laden with muscle it makes all those scary bulls look like cupcakes. That's the Belgian Blue, and

"Belgian Blues Will Blow Your Minds, These Cows Are Totally Ripped," Aaron Saenz, Singularity Hub, July 13, 2011. Reprinted by permission.

despite the breeds docility, it never fails to impress onlookers as a very frightening animal.

In [an audio clip] we hear about some of the amazing advantages associated with the Belgian Blue strain. They can have 40% or more additional edible muscle mass, most of which is lean meat! They gain weight well, and quickly, and produce high protein milk for their young. While they comprise a relatively small percentage of the international market, the meat itself is highly prized as its lean nature makes it healthier (and some say more tender and juicy as well).

What the breeder in the National Geographic video doesn't have time to outline is the physical problems associated with uninhibited muscle growth. The Belgian Blue and the Piedmontese, another breed with myostatin problems, are viable farm strains of cattle. They can live, reproduce, give milk, and be consumed with no risk to humans. To themselves, however, these Conan-looking cows are less friendly. They experience a wide range of health risks associated with their muscle—calves can develop enlarged tongues and stiff legs which make it difficult, if not impossible, to feed, leading to early death. Many of the cattle develop cardio-respiratory ailments. In almost all modern herds, Caesarean sections are common due to complications in pregnancy, and in some cases C-section rates have climbed to nearly 90% of all births!

Both the impressive bulk and health issues of the Belgian Blue have been maintained through the relatively simple technology of line breeding. Essentially, a very few bulls are selected to be the fathers for calves in all of the females. By choosing those bulls which clearly demonstrate the myostatin defect phenotype, breeders can make more and more of the muscled cattle. Once semen is collected from bulls (as the video so graciously shows us—eww) it can be tested and then used to impregnate cows through artificial insemination. Anecdotally it is suggested that most of the world's current Belgian Blue herds were derived from just three bulls and their descendants. While that may be an exaggeration, the truth is certainly that in efforts to perfect the breed very few male genetic lines are allowed to continue.

That's true for all types of cattle and livestock, really. Traditional selective breeding pushes us towards a narrower gene pool. It's unclear if that is going to get much worse or much better as modern genetic testing takes hold. We've already discussed how cheaper DNA tests are allowing cattle breeders to choose the absolute best bulls for line breeding. Those cheap tests mean that any rancher can now see if they have a prize bull. That may open up breeders to using new fathers, or it may simply replace the very small number of current stud bulls with a new, but equally small, generation of replacements.

Either way, what's good for cattle is slowly becoming good for humans. Though no one seems to want to phrase it in this way, humans are starting to adopt selective breeding habits and technologies. There are now several companies that sell genetic tests in association with in vitro fertilization (IVF) clinics. With good cause, I might add. Successful testing for Tay-Sachs has helped dramatically reduce the occurence of that disease in the US. Most of these newer genetic testing companies are looking to repeat that success for more than a hundred other genetic conditions. Wouldn't you want to know before you got pregnant if your children would be at high risk for crippling ailments? If you are a genetic carrier for such a disease then Preimplantation Genetic Diagnosis (PGD) can allow you to select fertilized embryos without the disease. IVF and PGD are giving us the tools necessary to, at least in terms of our own gametes, become selective breeders. Breeders informed with rudimentary genetic information, which is a step up from those Belgian farmers who first started propagating their mutant cows.

We've discussed before how genetically engineered animals are on the horizon and could be on our plates in the near future. The Belgian Blue's mutant myostatin gene variation has even been spliced into rainbow trout to give them more bulk (and thus more more worth as food). Animals are already being genetically engineered, and if work in primates is any indication, we're slowly approaching the time when scientists will be able to waltz inside a human embryo, tinker with its DNA, and get the child to come to term. That possibility, however, scares the sh*t out of most people, and angers the rest. The chances that human genetic engineering is going to have a smooth transition into becoming a popular technology is almost nil. Expect legal and social hurdles to abound. Hell, I wouldn't be surprised if armed conflict arose around this controversy as well. It could take decades before we accept such technology, though my bet is eventually that we will.

Meanwhile, modern sex powers on. PGD and IVF aren't universally excepted, but they aren't fueling riots either. Morally, they are a much more widely acceptable technology. Personally, I know a few IVF (possibly even PGD) kids and my world would be a lot poorer if they weren't around. I'm glad it's an option for parents.

But that doesn't keep it from being a stepping stone to some pretty amazing selective breeding opportunities that could give us the equivalent of designer babies even without genetic engineering. See the Belgian Blue? That's a single mutant gene that turned out to be helpful, and that simple breeding habit was propagated for more than a century. We've already seen human children who were born with the equivalent of the myostatin defect seen in the monstrous cattle. Picture a time when we discover other, relatively rare but potentially advantageous, genetic mutations. Imagine if everyone had the ability to comb through their sperm and find those mutant gametes with the desired traits you want. You could optimize your offspring—give yourself super babies with no genetic tampering required. Long before genetics is ready to replace it with something better, sexual reproduction is going to get more and more impressive thanks to modern technology.

I look forward to seeing all your Belgian Blue-like children in the future.

Genetic Engineering Can Fight Disease in Animals

Bill Pohlmeier and Alison Van Eenennaam

Bill Pohlmeier is the physiology lab manager at the University of Nebraska, Lincoln.

Alison Van Eenennaam is a cooperative extension specialist in animal genomics and biotechnology at the University of California, Davis.

A nimal disease is a major social and economic problem across the United States, and throughout the world. Diseases can lead to animal suffering and distress, reduced performance, and possibly even death. Infectious diseases have major negative effects on poultry and livestock production, both in terms of economics and on animal welfare. The costs of animal disease are estimated to be 35-50% of turnover within the livestock sector in developing countries, and 17% in the developed world. Often animal disease is fought through vaccination or the use of antibiotics. However, the use of antibiotic in animal agriculture is meeting increased disapproval among consumers. In addition to enhancing animal well-being, improving animal health has the added benefit of reducing the need for veterinary interventions and the use of antibiotics and other medicinal treatments.

Animal biotechnology offers a number of approaches to fight disease in animals. Firstly, through genetic selection, livestock producers can select for certain genetic variations which have been associated with disease resistance. Through careful selection, they can develop populations of animals that are less vulnerable to disease. Secondly, through genetic engineering, breeders can integrate disease resistance genes from new sources, allowing for improved animal health. Disease resistance benefits not only

"Potential Effects of Biotechnology on Animal Health and Well-being," by Bill Pohlmeier and Alison Van Eenennaam, Applications of Animal Biotechnology in Animal Health, January 2009. Reprinted by permission.

livestock producers and their animals, but consumers also benefit as a result of safer animal products in the market place, and a reduction in the incidence of human-transmissible diseases such as avian influenza. Cattle are one species that could benefit from selection for disease resistance. Major diseases affecting cattle include foot and mouth disease, mad cow disease, mastitis, shipping fever, and brucellosis.

Disease Resistance through Genetic Selection

One method to increase disease resistance in a population of animals is to select animals which show resistance to a disease to be the parents of future generations. In this way, animals with specific genetic variations associated with disease resistance can pass those genetics on to their offspring, thus increasing the likelihood that their offspring will be resistant to infection. It has long been known that mice carrying a certain version (allele) of the Mx gene show resistance to influenza infection,[1] with the certain allele responsible for resistance known as Mx1.[2] A homologous, or similar, Mx gene has been identified in swine.[3] In vitro studies reveal that certain forms of the swine Mx gene confer different levels of resistance to influenza infection,[4] and it is thought that future in vivo studies will reveal whether selection for a certain form of swine Mx gene results in influenza resistance within a swine population. Major diseases affecting pigs include foot and mouth disease, influenza, swine fever, respiratory and wasting diseases.

Chickens are a natural host for avian influenza. As such, influenza infection in chickens can lead to sickness and even death. As with mice and swine, an Mx gene has been identified in chickens.[5, 6] In vitro studies show that certain copies of the chicken Mx gene display different levels of antiviral activity,[7] suggesting that certain populations of chickens might be less susceptible to avian influenza infection, based on their genetic background. However, similar to swine, in vivo studies will be required to determine whether live chickens actually display resistance to influenza infection based on their copy of Mx. Chicken is another species that could benefit from increased disease resistance. Major diseases affecting chickens include avian influenza, Newcastle, and Marek's diseases.

Disease-resistant Genetically Engineered Animals

While selection for disease resistance in livestock species might prove to be a powerful tool for livestock producers, it is limited by the natural genetic variation present in the species being selected. Genetic engineering, on the other hand, allows for the introduction of novel genetic sequences into the species of interest and is not limited by species barriers as the genetic building blocks in all species are the same. The use of genetic engineering has long been suggested as a method to increase disease resistance in livestock,[8] and scientists are currently working on a number of different animal models which could be used to help livestock resist infection (Table 1).

Spongiform encephalopathies, such as scrapie in sheep, and Bovine Spongiform Encephalopathy (BSE) also known as "Mad Cow Disease" in cattle are neurodegenerative diseases caused by the misfolding of a prion protein. BSE has been linked to the human neurodegenerative disease called variant Creutzfeldt Jakob disease,[27, 28] and is thus a potential threat to human health. In a procedure known as gene knockout, scientists can target a specific gene in an organism and remove it. This technology was successfully used to "knockout" the gene which codes for the prion protein in goats,[9] sheep,[10] and cattle.[11, 12] In addition to generating livestock which are free from the threat of spongiform encephalopathies, these animals could be used as a "prion-free" source of biological products for use in human medicine. Transgenic goats carrying lentivectors that express siRNAs against the prion protein have been reported.[15] RNAi is a sequence-specific method to selectively knock down endogenous gene expression. It works by introducing transgenic homologous double-stranded gene constructs which enable the stable expression of small interfering (si)RNAs that constitutively suppress target gene expression.[29]

Table 1. Extant and envisioned application for the production of disease-resistant genetically engineered livestock.

EXTANT APPLICATIONS	SPECIES	GENE	APPROACH	REFERENCE
BSE resistance	Cattle, Sheep, Goats	Prion	Knockout	9-12
Mastitis resistance	Cattle	Lysostaphin	Transgene overexpression	13
Mastitis resistance	Cattle	Lactoferrin	Transgene overexpression	14
BSE resistance	Goat	Prion	RNAi transgene	15
Visna virus resistance	Sheep	Visna virus envelope gene	Transgene overexpression	16
Mastitis resistance	Goat	Lysozyme	Transgene overexpression	17, 18
GCH virus resistance	Grass Carp	Lactoferrin	Transgene overexpression	19
Bacterial resistance	Channel Catfish	Cecropin B gene	Transgene overexpression	20
ENVISIONED APPLICATIONS	SPECIES	GENE	APPROACH	REFERENCE
Suppressing infectious pathogens	Various	RNA viruses (eg. foot and mouth, fowl plague, swine fever)	RNAi	21, 22
Coronavirus resistance	Swine	Aminopeptidase N	RNAi / Knockout	23
Avian flu resistance	Poultry	Avian influenza	RNAi	24, 25
Brucellosis resistance	Cattle	NRAMP1	Transgene overexpression	26

This approach may be a highly efficient approach to generate GE animals with targeted gene knockouts in the future, including GE animals that can knockdown infections caused by important contagious RNA viruses such as foot and mouth disease, classic swine fever, and fowl plague.[21]

Mastitis, or the infection of the mammary gland, is a disease which costs the US Dairy industry ~$2 Billion a year.[30] In an effort to reduce the effect of mastitis, scientists have developed genetically engineered cattle which are resistant to mastitis infection.[13] These cattle contain a transgene which encodes for the protein lysostaphin, which cleaves the cell wall of the bacteria which cause mastitis. Transgenic cattle produce the lysostaphin transgene in their mammary gland, which then breaks down infectious bacteria present within the gland and results in a healthier mammary gland. Similar studies using a human lysozyme transgene have demonstrated that the direction of transgene expression to the mammary gland in goats can result in reduced mastitis-causing bacteria.[17] The benefits of genetically engineered animals with disease resistance are two-fold. Firstly, they result in a healthier mammary gland, thus reducing pain and discomfort in the animals. Secondly, with reduced mammary infection, the milk, and milk products from these animals are going to be healthier, as harmful bacteria are reduced.

Research using genetic engineering to improve disease resistance is also being conducted on aquaculture species. Transgenic catfish have been developed which contain the cecropin B gene from the moth *Hyalophora cecropia*.[20] Cecropin is a small molecule that has shown anti-microbial properties, specifically against many of the bacteria that are harmful to catfish. When transgenic catfish were challenged with a form of E coli, statistically more transgenic fish survived than their non-transgenic counterparts, suggesting that expression of the transgene does indeed confer disease resistance. A disease with the potential to be treated through genetic engineering is brucellosis. Brucellosis, caused by the Brucella bacteria, is a zoonotic disease, meaning it can be ready passed between animals of different species. The animal population in and around the Yellowstone region in northwest Wyoming provides a prime example of how easily brucellosis can be spread. A number of large animal species (American Bison, Elk, etc.) in this area suffer from brucellosis.

When these infected animals come into contact with grazing cattle, the disease is readily passed. Cattle infected with brucellosis often suffer abortions, reduced fertility, and decreased milk production. In addition, brucellosis can also be passed to humans (known as undulant fever) who come into contact with infected animals, and the results can be severe. Recently a link has been established between brucellosis resistance and a variant of the bovine NRAMP1 gene.[26] Through genetic engineering, cattle could be produced which highly express the disease resistant version of NRAMP1, thus increasing their resistance to brucellosis.

A major goal of livestock and poultry breeding programs continues to be the identification of disease resistance genes, and genes that enhance immune response. There are a variety of animal biotechnologies that could be used to assist in the pursuit of this goal. Genomic selection and advanced breeding programs provide methods to identify naturally-occurring variation in disease-resistance attributes, while genetic engineering provides an approach to introduce new sources of disease resistance genes into populations. Collectively these technologies have the potential to align animal production systems with sustainability goals such as improved animal well-being due to lower disease incidence, reduced human health risk from zoonotic diseases (e.g. Mad Cow Disease, Avian Influenza, Brucellosis), and the production of safer food due to the decreased use of antibiotics and other medicinal treatments.

PEER-REVIEWED REFERENCES CITED

1. Horisberger,M.A. & Hochkeppel,H.K. An interferon-induced mouse protein involved in the mechanism of resistance to influenza viruses. Its purification to homogeneity and characterization by polyclonal antibodies. *J. Biol. Chem.* **260**, 1730-1733 (1985).

2. Staeheli,P., Grob,R., Meier,E., Sutcliffe,J.G., & Haller,O. Influenza virus-susceptible mice carry Mx genes with a large deletion or a nonsense mutation. *Mol. Cell Biol.* **8**, 4518-4523 (1988).

3. Muller,M., Winnacker,E.L., & Brem,G. Molecular cloning of porcine Mx cDNAs: new members of a family of interferon-inducible proteins with homology to GTP-binding proteins. *J. Interferon Res.* **12**, 119-129 (1992).

4. Palm,M., Leroy,M., Thomas,A., Linden,A., & Desmecht,D. Differential anti-influenza activity among allelic variants at the Sus scrofa Mx1 locus. *J. Interferon Cytokine Res.* **27**, 147-155 (2007).

5. Schumacher,B., Bernasconi,D., Schultz,U., & Staeheli,P. The chicken Mx promoter contains an ISRE motif and confers interferon inducibility to a reporter gene in chick and monkey cells. *Virology* **203**, 144-148 (1994).

6. Bernasconi,D., Schultz,U., & Staeheli,P. The interferon-induced Mx protein of chickens lacks antiviral activity. *J. Interferon Cytokine Res.* **15**, 47-53 (1995).

7. Ko,J.H. et al. Polymorphisms and the differential antiviral activity of the chicken Mx gene. *Genome Res.* **12**, 595-601 (2002).

8. Muller,M. & Brem,G. Intracellular, genetic or congenital immunisation—transgenic approaches to increase disease resistance of farm animals. *J. Biotechnol.* **44**, 233-242 (1996).

9. Yu,G.H. et al. Functional disruption of the prion protein gene in cloned goats. *Journal of General Virology* **87**, 1019-1027 (2006).

10. Denning,C. et al. Deletion of the alpha(1,3) galactosyl transferase (GGTA1) gene and the prion protein (PrP) gene in sheep. *Nature Biotechnology* **19**, 559-562 (2001).

11. Richt,J.A. et al. Production and characterization of prion protein-deficient cattle. *Transgenic Research* **16**, 842-843 (2007).

12. Richt,J.A. et al. Production of cattle lacking prion protein. *Nature Biotechnology* **25**, 132-138 (2007).

13. Wall,R.J. et al. Genetically enhanced cows resist intramammary Staphylococcus aureus infection. *Nature Biotechnology* **23**, 445-451 (2005).

14. van Berkel,P.H. et al. Large scale production of recombinant human lactoferrin in the milk of transgenic cows. *Nat Biotechnol.* **20**, 484-487 (2002).

15. Golding,M.C., Long,C.R., Carmell,M.A., Hannon,G.J., & Westhusin,M.E. Suppression of prion protein in livestock by RNA interference. *Proceedings of the National Academy of Sciences of the United States of America* **103**, 5285-5290 (2006).

16. Clements,J.E. et al. Development of transgenic sheep that express the visna virus envelope gene. *Virology* **200**, 370-380 (1994).

17. Maga,E.A., Cullor,J.S., Smith,W., Anderson,G.B., & Murray,J.D. Human lysozyme expressed in the mammary gland of transgenic dairy goats can inhibit the growth of bacteria that cause mastitis and the cold-spoilage of milk. *Foodborne Pathog. Dis.* **3**, 384-392 (2006).

18. Maga,E.A. et al. Production and processing of milk from transgenic goats expressing human lysozyme in the mammary gland. *Journal of Dairy Science* **89**, 518-524 (2006).

19. Zhong,J.Y., Wang,Y.P., & Zhu,Z.Y. Introduction of the human lactoferrin gene into grass carp (Ctenopharyngodon idellus) to increase resistance against GCH virus. *Aquaculture* **214**, 93- 101 (2002).

20. Dunham,R.A. et al. Enhanced bacterial disease resistance of transgenic channel catfish Ictalurus punctatus possessing cecropin genes. *Marine Biotechnology* **4**, 338-344 (2002).

21. Clark,J. & Whitelaw,B. A future for transgenic livestock. *Nat. Rev. Genet.* **4**, 825-833 (2003).

22. Whitelaw,C.B. & Sang,H.M. Disease-resistant genetically modified animals. *Rev Sci. Tech* **24**, 275-283 (2005).

23. Schwegmann-Wessels,C., Zimmer,G., Laude,H., Enjuanes,L., & Herrler,G. Binding of transmissible gastroenteritis coronavirus to cell surface sialoglycoproteins. *Journal of Virology* **76**, 6037-6043 (2002).

24. Sang,H. Transgenic chickens—methods and potential applications. *Trends Biotechnol.* **12**, 415- 420 (1994).

25. Tompkins,S.M., Lo,C.Y., Tumpey,T.M., & Epstein,S.L. Protection against lethal influenza virus challenge by RNA interference in vivo. *Proceedings of the National Academy of Sciences of the United States of America* **101**, 8682-8686 (2004).

26. Barthel,R. et al. Stable transfection of the bovine NRAMP1 gene into murine RAW264.7 cells: effect on Brucella abortus survival. *Infect. Immun.* **69**, 3110-3119 (2001).

27. Hill,A.F. et al. The same prion strain causes vCJD and BSE. *Nature* **389**, 448-50, 526 (1997).

28. Bruce,M.E. et al. Transmissions to mice indicate that "new variant" CJD is caused by the BSE agent. *Nature* **389**, 498-501 (1997).

29. Martin,S.E. & Caplen,N.J. Applications of RNA Interference in Mammalian Systems.* *Annual Review of Genomics and Human Genetics* **8**, 81-108 (2007).

30. Sordillo,L.M. & Streicher,K.L. Mammary gland immunity and mastitis susceptibility. *J. Mammary. Gland. Biol. Neoplasia.* **7**, 135-146 (2002).

Genetically Modifying Animals Causes Serious Health Problems

Compassion in World Farming

Compassion in World Farming is a nonprofit organization headquartered in the UK that campaigns and lobbies to improve the welfare of livestock.

Scientific research shows that cloning and genetic manipulation (GM) entail serious health and welfare problems for cloned and GM animals as well as for the surrogate mothers who carry them to birth.

Cloning and GM would take agriculture in the wrong direction, perpetuating industrial farming. This involves the use of animals selected for such high yields and growth rates that they are vulnerable to damaging health problems. Cloning and GM are out of step with the growing recognition of the need to respect animals as sentient beings.

NEW REPORT

To gain the most up-to-date knowledge on the production and use of cloned and genetically-engineered animals, Compassion in World Farming commissioned a report by animal welfare experts, Professor Don Broom and Dr Richard Kirkden from Cambridge University.[1] The report, *The Welfare of Genetically Modified and Cloned Animals Used for Food*, provides a comprehensive assessment of recent work in this field.*

The full report shows that:

- high rates of pre- and post-natal mortality and poor health are common in cloned cattle and sheep

---

"Cloning and Genetic Engineering of Animals for Food Production," CIWF.org. Reprinted by permission.

- the health problems experienced by these animals include breathing difficulties, heart function insufficiency, kidney problems and an increased susceptibility to infectious disease
- the production of genetically-engineered animals can also involve the suffering and death of many animals.

Cloning

Cloning aims to produce genetically identical copies of an animal.

The cloning process

The most commonly used procedure is somatic cell nuclear transfer (SCNT). This involves collecting a cell from the animal that is to be cloned (the "donor cell") and removing an egg cell from another animal. This cell is enucleated, i.e. its genetic material is removed. The donor cell and the egg cell are then fused by an electrical pulse and from this a cloned embryo is developed. This is implanted into a surrogate mother (dam).

In sheep and pigs, the transfer of the embryo into the surrogate mother is performed by a surgical procedure. In cattle, embryo transfer is sufficiently stressful that UK legislation requires a general or epidural anaesthetic.

Impact on health and welfare of surrogate dams

The European Food Safety Authority (EFSA) states that there is an increase in pregnancy failure in cattle and pigs who are carrying a clone and increased frequencies of difficult birth, especially in cattle.[2] This, together with the increased size of cloned offspring, makes Caesarean sections more frequent in cattle carrying a clone than with conventional pregnancies.

Impact on health and welfare of clones

EFSA has concluded: "The health and welfare of a significant proportion of clones ... have been found to be adversely affected, often severely and with a fatal outcome."[3] Most cloned foetuses die during pregnancy or birth. Only 6-15% of cloned cattle embryos and about 6% of pig embryos are born alive . Many of these die early in life from problems such as cardiovascular failure, respiratory difficulties and defective immune systems. Of those born alive, up to 22% of cloned calves, 25% of cloned piglets and 50% of cloned lambs die before weaning.[5]

Process of Cloning by Somatic Cell Nuclear Transfer

Cells are collected from
the donor animal

Egg cell is collected from
dead or live animal

↓

↓

Donor cell
is cultured

Egg cell is enucleated
(removal of the nucleus)

↓

↓

Donor cell is transferred into enucleated egg.
Cells then fused by an electrical pulse.

↓

Cloned embryo transferred to surrogate mother

↓

Birth of clone

European Group on Ethics

The Opinion of the European Group on Ethics (EGE) in Science and New Technologies concluded that: "Considering the current level of suffering and health problems of surrogate dams and animal clones, the EGE has doubts as to whether cloning animals for food supply is ethically justified."[6]

Use of offspring of clones on-farm

Clones will primarily be used as elite breeding animals. It is their offspring that will be farmed for meat or milk.

The likelihood is that cloning will primarily be used to produce copies of the highest yielding dairy cows and fastest growing pigs. However, traditional genetic selection has already led to major health problems for such animals. EFSA has concluded that "*genetic selection for high milk yield is the major factor causing poor welfare, in particular health problems, in dairy cows"*[7] and that genetic selection of pigs for rapid growth has led to leg disorders and cardiovascular malfunction.[8] The use of the offspring of clones on farms is likely to entrench the use of animals chosen for extreme production traits and risks perpetuating the health problems associated with such traits.

Is the incidence of pathologies and mortality declining?

Some researchers claim they are managing to reduce the incidence of ill-health and mortalities involved in cloning. A considerable body of evidence suggests that this is not the case.

In 2012 EFSA stated that no new information has become available that would lead it to reconsider the conclusions in its 2008 Opinion on the animal health and welfare aspects of cloning.[9] Unacceptable death rates of the animals involved have forced AgResearch, a leading New Zealand research organisation, to end its SCNT cloning trials.[10] A Japanese survey revealed that survival rates of transferred cloned bovine embryos and cloned calves had not improved—indeed had deteriorated—over a decade (1998–2007).[11]

Genetic Engineering

Farm animals are being genetically engineered for various purposes including enhanced growth rates, increased disease resistance and altered meat and milk composition.

Genetic engineering involves the insertion into an animal of genes from another species or extra genes from the same species. Alternatively it can entail the manipulation or knocking-out of an animal's own genes.

Enhanced growth rates

Animals that have been genetically engineered for faster growth have suffered from harmful side-effects. The production of fast-growing GM animals is most advanced in the case of farmed fish. This has led to deformities, feeding and breathing difficulties, reduced swimming abilities and lower tolerance to disease.[12]

Increased disease resistance

Conferring improved disease resistance on animals appears to be benign. However, the UN Food and Agriculture Organization points out that industrial livestock production plays an important part in the emergence and spread of diseases.[13] The proper way to address such diseases is to keep animals in less intensive systems. Good hygiene, husbandry and housing rather than genetic engineering should be used to prevent the diseases that stem from factory farming.

Altered meat and milk composition

Researchers point to the health benefits of tackling rising levels of obesity and cardiovascular disease in humans by genetically engineering animals to produce lower levels of saturated fats and higher levels of beneficial omega-3 fatty acids. However, the incidence of these problems can be reduced by improving our diet. A major study concluded that a 30% decrease in intake of saturated fats from animal sources in the UK could reduce heart disease by 15%.[14] Reduced levels of saturated fat and improved levels of omega-3 fatty acids can be achieved by replacing factory farmed chicken and grain-fed beef with free-range chicken (especially slower growing breeds) and pasture-fed beef.[15]

Policy Recommendations

In light of the adverse impact of cloning and GM on animal health and welfare, cloning and GM animals should not play any part in European farming.

The EU Should Prohibit:

- the cloning or genetic engineering of animals for food production
- the use of clones, GM animals and their offspring in the EU; this will make it pointless to import semen and embryos of clones and GM animals
- the sale of food from clones and GM animals

- the sale of food from the offspring of clones and GM animals. At the very least, such food should be labelled.

* This work was made possible by a grant from the World Society for the Protection of Animals (WSPA) and the full report is available to download from ciwf.org/cloningreport.

REFERENCES

1. Broom, D. and Kirkden, R., 2012. Welfare of Genetically Modified and Cloned Animals Used for Food.
2. EFSA, 2008. Scientific Opinion of the Scientific Committee on a request from the European Commission on Food Safety, Animal Health and Welfare and Environmental Impact of Animals derived from Cloning by Somatic Cell Nucleus Transfer (SCNT) and their Offspring and Products Obtained from those Animals. *EFSA Journal*, 767: 1-49.
3. *Ibid*
4. EFSA, 2012. Update on the state of play of Animal Health and Welfare and Environmental Impact of Animals derived from SCNT Cloning and their Offspring, and Food Safety of Products Obtained from those Animals. *EFSA Journal*, 10(7):2794.
5. Broom, D. and Kirkden, R., 2012. Welfare of Genetically Modified and Cloned Animals Used for Food.
6. European Group on Ethics in Science and New Technologies, 2008. Ethical aspects of animal cloning for food supply. Opinion No. 23.
7. EFSA, 2009. Scientific Opinion on the overall effects of farming systems on dairy cow welfare and disease. *EFSA Journal*, 1143, 1-38.
8. EFSA, 2007. Animal health and welfare in fattening pigs in relation to housing and husbandry. *EFSA Journal*, 564, 1-14.
9. As 4
10. Reported in New Zealand press and confirmed as accurate by New Zealand Ministry of Agriculture.
11. Watanabe S. and Nagai T., 2011. Survival of embryos and calves derived from somatic cell nuclear transfer in cattle: a nationwide survey in Japan. *Animal Science Journal*, 82, 360-365.
12. Compassion in World Farming and WSPA, 2007. Closed Waters: The welfare of farmed atlantic salmon, rainbow trout, atlantic cod & atlantic halibut.
13. Otte, J. *et al*, 2007. Industrial Livestock Production and Global Health Risks. Pro-Poor Livestock Policy Initiative.
14. Friel *et al*, 2009. Public health benefits of strategies to reduce greenhouse-gas emissions: food and agriculture. *The Lancet*, 374 (9706), 2016 – 2025.
15. Compassion in World Farming, 2012. Nutritional benefits of higher welfare animal products. ciwf.org/nutrition.

Many Issues with GM Animals Still Debated

Yourgenome.org

Yourgenome.org is a source of information about genetics sponsored by the Public Engagement team at the Wellcome Genome Campus in the UK.

Genetic engineering refers to the direct manipulation of an organism's genes to alter or enhance certain characteristics.

The number of genetically modified animals used in agriculture has increased significantly in recent years. Researchers have genetically engineered a number of mammals, from laboratory animals to farm animals, as well as birds, fish and insects.

The most widely used genetically modified animals are laboratory animals, such as the fruitfly (*Drosophila*) and mice. Genetically engineered animals enable scientists to gain an insight into basic biological processes and the relationships between mutations and disease.

However, farm animals, such as sheep, goats and cows, can also be genetically modified to enhance specific characteristics. These can include milk production and disease resistance, as well as improving the nutritional value of the products they are farmed for. For example, cows, goats and sheep have been genetically engineered to express specific proteins in their milk.

The majority of work on genetically modified farm animals is still in the research phase and is yet to be used commercially. Below are some of the advantages and disadvantages associated with genetically modifying animals for agriculture, divided up into four key areas:

"Is it ethical to genetically modify farm animals for agriculture?" Debate, yourgenome.org, Reprinted by permission.

- Do the benefits of genetically modified farm animals outweigh the risks?
- Is genetic modification of farm animals ethical?
- Is it morally acceptable to genetically modify farm animals?
- Is there a thorough regulatory process for genetic modification of farm animals?

Do the benefits of genetically modified farm animals outweigh the risks?

Yes

- Genetic engineering holds great potential in many fields, including agriculture, medicine and industry.
- Genetic modification can increase the yield from farm animals, for example cows can be engineered to produce more milk for the same size of herd.
- Genetically modified farm animals are being used to produce important medicinal products, such as antibodies, in large quantities. These products can be used for the treatment of many different human conditions. The current production system for such products is donated human blood, which is in limited supply due to a lack of donors.
- Sheep and goats can be modified to produce medicinal products in their milk. This has no negative impact on the animal but the product can help to treat human diseases.

No

- The transfer of genetic material from one species to another raises potentially serious health issues for animals and humans.
- There is a risk that new diseases from genetically engineered animals could be spread to non-genetically engineered animals, and even humans.
- In many cases, selective breeding is just as effective as genetic engineering and doesn't carry the same risks.

- We don't yet know if eating the products of genetically modified animals could potentially harm us.

Is genetic modification of farm animals ethical?

Yes

- Genetic engineering is a logical continuation of selective breeding, which has been done by humans for thousands of years.
- Genetic engineering of animals is strictly controlled by animal cruelty legislations in many countries and is always carefully scrutinised by teams of experts before being approved for wider use.

No

- Many of the embryos that undergo genetic engineering procedures do not survive.
- Genetic modification can put animals at risk of harm. For example, transgenic pigs were found to be arthritic, partially blind and infertile when a human growth hormone was inserted into their genomes to make them grow faster.

Is it morally acceptable to genetically modify farm animals?

Yes

- Not all genetic engineering directly benefits humans. Some genetic engineering is to improve resistance of livestock to disease, for example, bovine spongiform encephalopathy ("mad cow disease") in cattle. It can also be used to remove characteristics that cause injury, for example, selecting for cattle without horns.
- Animals have been used to help humans for millennia. Many would say that human lives are of higher moral value than animal lives.

- The percentage of genetically modified farm animals is tiny compared to the number of animals slaughtered for humans to eat. This practice is widely seen as morally acceptable.

No

- Research could use other organisms such as plants and bacteria to mass produce therapies for human medicine. For example, genetically engineered cereal grains to produce human proteins.
- The cost to the animal always outweighs the benefits as, by carrying out genetic engineering, we are violating their rights
- Genetic engineering often involves modifying animals for reasons that have no benefit for that species, and could potentially cause them pain and discomfort.
- We shouldn't be attempting to "play God." Life should not be regarded as a product that can be altered and played with for economic benefit.

Is there a thorough regulatory process for genetic modification of farm animals?

Yes

- It has been suggested that, as a rule, genetically engineered animals should be no worse off than the equivalent stock would be if they were not genetically engineered.
- The Animal Welfare Act, a federal law passed in the UK in 1966, requires all entities looking to carry out research with animals to have their programme reviewed before they go ahead, have veterinary care programmes in place and staff that are qualified to care for live animals.
- The UK Home Office Animals (Scientific Procedures) Act 1986 has set out guidelines for research involving animals.
- The FDA (Food and Drug Administration) in the USA regulates genetic engineering with animals and their products under the new animal drug provisions of the Federal Food,

Drug and Cosmetic Act (FFDCA). It helps monitor and maintain certain standards, including input from the public, when it comes to genetically engineering animals.

- The "new animal drug" provisions of the FFDCA focuses on whether the new animal drug is safe for the animal and if it is effective. If the drug is for a food-producing animal it also focuses on whether the resulting food is safe to eat.

No

- Genetic engineering of animals is a relatively new practice and is mainly used in research. As a result regulations for its use in farming are minimal.
- For regulations that have been put in place for the use of animals in research, it is often unclear how they would be applied to genetic engineering of farm animals and few guidelines refer to it directly.

Organizations to Contact

The editors have compiled the following list of organizations concerned with the issues debated in this book. The descriptions are derived from materials provided by the organizations. All have publications or information available for interested readers. This list was compiled on the date of publication of the present volume; the information provided here may change. Be aware that many organizations take several weeks or longer to respond to inquiries, so allow as much time as possible.

American Society for Human Genetics (ASHG)
9650 Rockville Pike
Bethesda, MD 20814-3998
(301) 634-7300
email: society@ashg.org
website: http://www.ashg.org

The American Society of Human Genetics (ASHG) is the primary professional membership organization for human genetics specialists worldwide. ASHG provides forums for advancing genetic research, improving genetics education, and promoting responsible scientific policies. ASHG publishes the *American Journal of Human Genetics* and the electronic newsletter *SNP-IT*.

American Society of Law, Medicine & Ethics (ASLME)
765 Commonwealth Avenue, Suite 1634
Boston, MA 02215
(617) 262-4990
email: infor@aslme.org
website: http://www.aslme.org

The American Society of Law, Medicine & Ethics (ASLME) is a nonprofit educational organization focused on the intersection of law, medicine, and ethics. ASLME provides a forum for the exchange of ideas to protect public health, reduce health disparities, promote quality of care, and facilitate dialogue on emerging science. ASLME publishes the *Journal of Law, Medicine & Ethics* and *American Journal of Law & Medicine*.

Biotechnology Innovation Organization (BIO)

1201 Maryland Avenue SW, Suite 900
Washington, DC 20024
(202) 962-9200
email: info@bio.org
website: http://www.bio.org

The Biotechnology Innovation Organization (BIO) is a trade association representing biotechnology companies, academic institutions, state biotechnology centers, and related organizations worldwide. Its members are involved in the research and development of innovative health care, agricultural, industrial, and environmental biotechnology products. BIO publishes *BIOtechNOW* and the *BIO Newsletter*.

Center for Food Safety (CFS)

660 Pennsylvania Avenue SE, Suite 301
Washington, DC 20003
(202) 547-9359
email: office@centerforfoodsafety.org
website: http://www.centerforfoodsafety.org

Center for Food Safety (CFS) is a nonprofit public interest and environmental advocacy organization It works to protect human health and the environment by curbing the use of harmful food production technologies and by promoting organic and other forms of sustainable agriculture. CFS also educates consumers concerning the definition of organic food and products. CFS uses legal actions, groundbreaking scientific and policy reports, books and other educational materials, market pressure, and grass roots campaigns. CFS educates consumers concerning the definition of organic food and products. Available on its website are fact sheets, newsletters, reports, and policy statements on food and agricultural issues.

Center for Genetics and Society (CGS)

1122 University Avenue, Suite 100
Berkeley, CA 94702
(510) 665-7760
email: info@geneticsandsociety.org
website: http://www.geneticsandsociety.org

The Center for Genetics and Society is a nonprofit information and public affairs organization working to encourage responsible uses and effective oversight of human genetic and reproductive technologies and other emerging technologies. CGS works with a network of scientists, health professionals, and civil society leaders to oppose applications of new human genetic and reproductive technology applications that objectify and commodify human life and threaten to divide human society. CGS publishes *Biopolitical Times* and *Biopolitical Views & News*, available on its website.

Council for Responsible Genetics (CRG)

5 Upland Road, Suite 3
Cambridge, MA 02140
(617) 868-0870
email: crg@gene-watch.org
website: http://www.councilforresponsiblegenetics.org

The Council for Responsible Genetics is a nonprofit, non-governmental organization that fosters public debate about the social, ethical, and environmental implications of genetic technologies. CRG works through the media and concerned citizens to distribute accurate information on emerging issues in biotechnology. CRG also publishes a bimonthly magazine, *GeneWatch*, which monitors biotechnology's social, ethical, and environmental consequences.

Ethics and Public Policy Center (EPPC)
1730 M Street NW, Suite 910
Washington, DC 20036
(202) 682-1200
email: ethics@eppc.org
website: http://www.eppc.org

The Ethics and Public Policy Center (EPPC) is dedicated to applying the Judeo-Christian moral tradition to critical issues of public policy. EPPC defends and promotes our nation's founding principles—respect for the inherent dignity of the human person, individual freedom and responsibility, justice, the rule of law, and limited government. Its website provides a searchable database of commentaries by its scholars.

Food & Water Watch
1616 P Street NW, Suite 300
Washington, DC 20036
(202) 683-2500
email: info@fwwatch.org
website: http://www.foodandwaterwatch.org

Food & Water Watch is a public interest organization that promotes policies that lead to healthy food, safe and affordable drinking water, and sustainable energy. Its website provides a searchable policy and research library of reports, fact sheets, and case studies on such topic as GMOs and food safety.

Genetics Society of America (GSA)
9650 Rockville Pike
Bethesda, MD 20814-3998
(301) 634-7300
email: society@genetics-gsa.org
website: http://www.genetics-gsa.org

The mission of the Genetics Society of America (GSA) is to deepen the public's understanding of the living world by advancing the field of genetics. It fosters an international community of geneticists, educates students and the public, communicates new discoveries, and advocates for the continued support of genetics research. The GSA publishes two journals: *GENETICS*, and *G3: Genes|Genomes|Genetics.*

Institute for Responsible Technology
PO Box 469
Fairfield, IA 52556
(641) 209-1765
email: info@responsibletechnology.org
website: http://www.responsibletechnology.org

The Institute for Responsible Technology works to educate policy makers and the public about the dangers of genetically modified organisms (GMOs). The organization investigates and reports the impact of genetically modified food on health, environment, the economy, and agriculture, as well as the problems associated with current research, regulating, corporate practices, and reporting. The website provides reports, fact sheets, and multimedia presentations on the topic of GMOs.

International Centre for Genetic Engineering
Science Park
Padriciano 99
34149 Trieste, Italy
email: icgeb@icgeb.org
website: http://www.icgeb.org/home.html

This organization provides information regarding research in molecular biology and biotechnology that can meet the needs of the developing world. It focuses on biomedicine, crop improvement, environmental protection, and biopesticide production. Its website provides the results of its research and articles published in major scientific journals.

National Academies of Sciences, Engineering, and Medicine
500 Fifth Street NW
Washington, DC 20001
(202) 334-2000
email: worldwidewebfeedback@nas.edu
website: http://www.nationalacademies.org

These academies were established by the US government to provide scientific information and resources to members of Congress and the public. Among its areas of interest are agriculture, health and medicine, engineering and physical sciences, and policy and global affairs. Its website provides a searchable database of current and past research projects.

National Human Genome Research Institute (NHGRI)
National Institutes of Health
Building 31, Room 4B09
31 Center Drive, MSC 2152
9000 Rockville Pike
Bethesda, MD 20892-2152
(301) 402-0911
website: https://www.genome.gov

The National Human Genome Research Institute (NHGRI) was developed in collaboration with the United States Department of Energy to map the human genome. It established the Division of Intramural Research to apply genome technologies to the study of specific diseases and the genetic components of complex disorders. Its website contains many tools to facilitate the pace of biomedical research, including resources for educators, scientists, and journalists.

Union of Concerned Scientists
Two Brattle Square
Cambridge, MA 02138-3780
(617) 547-5552
website: http://www.ucsusa.org

The Union of Concerned Scientists works to build a safe and healthy world by encouraging scientific, evidence-based decision making at local, state, national, and international levels. It has played key roles in developing renewable energy sources and protection for rainforests. Its website contains blogs, publications, and reports on major environmental projects worldwide.

US Food and Drug Administration (FDA)
10903 New Hampshire Avenue
Silver Spring, MD 20993
(888) 463-6332
website: http://www.fda.gov

The Food and Drug Administration (FDA) is an agency within the US Department of Health and Human Services. The FDA is responsible for protecting public health by assuring food and drug safety. Its website provides resources and libraries on food safety, nutrition, food-relation regulations, and drug safety and research.

Bibliography

Books

Emily Anthes — *Frankenstein's Cat: Cuddling Up to Biotech's Brave New Beasts.* New York, NY: Scientific American/Farrar, Straus and Giroux, 2013.

Michael Burgan — *Genetic Engineering: Science, Technology, and Engineering* (Calling All Innovators). New York, NY: Scholastic, 2016.

Nessa Carey — *The Epigenetics Revolution.* New York, NY: Columbia University Press, 2012.

George Church and Edward Regis — *Regenesis: How Synthetic Biology Will Reinvent Nature and Ourselves.* New York, NY: Basic Books, 2012.

Marina Cohen — *Genetic Engineering* (Let's Relate to Genetics). New York, NY: Crabtree Publishing, 2010.

Steven Druker and Jane Goodall — *Altered Genes, Twisted Truth: How the Venture to Genetically Engineer Our Food Has Subverted Science, Corrupted Government, and Systematically Deceived the Public.* Salt Lake City, UT: Clear River Press, 2015.

Lillian Forman — *Genetically Modified Foods* (Essential Viewpoints). Edina, MN: ABDO Publishing, 2010.

Eve Hartman and Wendy Meshbesher — *What Are the Issues with Genetic Technology?* Chicago, IL: Raintree, 2012.

John T. Lang — *What's So Controversial About Genetically Modified Food?* London, UK: Reaktion Books, 2016.

Steven Lipkin and Jon Luoma — *The Age of Genomes: Tales from the Front Line.* Boston, MA: Beacon Press, 2016.

Salah E. Mahgoub — *Genetically Modified Foods: Basics, Applications, and Controversy,* London, UK: CRC Press, 2016.

Siddhartha Mukherjee — *The Gene: An Intimate History*. New York, NY: Scribner, 2016.

Kathy Wilson Peacock — *Biotechnology and Genetic Engineering* (Global Issues). New York, NY: Facts on File, 2010.

Steven Potter — *Designer Genes: A New Era in the Evolution of Man*. New York, NY: Random House, 2010.

Claire Robinson and Michael Antoniou — *GMO Myths and Truths*. London, UK: Earth Open Source, 2015.

Tara Rodden Robinson — *Genetics for Dummies*. Hoboken, NJ: Wiley Publishing, Inc., 2010.

Josh Schonwald — *The Taste of Tomorrow: Dispatches from the Future of Food*. New York, NY: Harper, 2012.

Marcus Wohlsen — *Biopunk: Kitchen-counter Scientists Hack the Software of Life*. New York, NY: Current, 2011.

Periodicals and Internet Sources

Jacqueline Adams — "Can Science Save Your Orange Juice?" *Science World*, Vol. 71, Issue 11, April 13, 2015, pp. 14–17.

Judith Benz-Schwarzburg and Arianna Ferrari — "Super-muscly Pigs Trading Ethics for Efficiency," *Issues in Science & Technology*, Vol. 32, Issue 3, Spring 2016, pp. 29–32.

Rachel Ehrenberg — "GMOs Under Scrutiny," *Science News*, Vol. 189, Issue 3, February 6, 2016, pp. 22–27.

Ferris Jabr — "Building Tastier Fruits & Veggies," *Scientific American*, Vol. 311, Issue 1, July 2014, pp. 56–61.

Melinda Wenner Moyer — "Infant Possibilities," *Popular Science*, Vol. 285, Issue 2, August 2014, pp. 50–85.

Russell Powell — "The Evolutionary Biological Implications of Human Genetic Engineering," *Journal of Medicine & Philosophy*, Vol. 37, Issue 3, June 2012, pp. 204–225.

William Powell — "The American Chestnut's Genetic Rebirth," *Scientific American*, Vol. 310, Issue 3, March 2014, pp. 68–73.

Antonio Regalado — "Engineering the Perfect Baby," *MIT Technology Review*, May/June 2015.

Tina Hesman Saey — "Gene Drives Unleashed," *Science News*, Vol. 188, Issue 12, December 12, 2015, pp. 16–22.

Index

R

reproductive cloning, 16, 26, 46–47,
49–50, 54, 55, 56, 57–58, 59, 60,
61, 72, 74, 75, 76
explanation of, 48
research animals, explanation of,
116
research cloning. *See*
therapeutic cloning
Roundup, 107, 109
Rubinsky, Boris, 25

S

Saenz, Aaron, 128–131
Sauer, Mark, 42
Savulescu, Julian, 37–40
Seed, Richard, 78
selective breeding, 14, 128, 130, 131,
147
Serbulea, Mihaela, 46–53
severe combined immunodeficiency,
28
Shiva, Vandana, 112
Silver, Lee M., 19, 20
Smith, Jeffrey, 106–110
somatic cell nuclear transfer
(SCNT), 47, 56, 57, 58, 61, 63–64,
72, 73, 74, 75, 76, 77, 141, 142, 143
somatic embryogenesis, 94, 95, 96
Stock, Gregory, 22, 24, 25
synthetic seeds, 95–97

T

Taylor, Michael, 108
therapeutic cloning, 16, 47, 55, 56,
59, 60, 61, 75, 76
explanation of, 16, 48, 50, 58
Tobin, Brendan, 46–53

U

UNESCO, 36, 46, 47
Union of Concerned Scientists, 109
United Nations, 55, 56, 85, 123, 144
United States Department of State,
54–62
United States Food and Drug
Administration, 42, 107–108,
116–127, 149
Universal Declaration on the
Human Genome and Human
Rights, 46–47

V

Van Eenennaam, Alison, 132–139

W

Waldman, Paul, 41–44
Watson, James, 22
Wechsler, Seth J., 98–105
*Welfare of Genetically Modified and
Cloned Animals Used for Food,
The,* 140
Wilmut, Ian, 72, 75
World Health Organization, 82–92,
112

X

xenotransplant animals, explanation
of, 117

Y

Yourgenome.org, 146–150